CRINGE-FREE EVANGELISM

Cringe-Free Evangelism

Finding a Way to Witness That is Right for You

Helen T. Boursier

Hodder & Stoughton
LONDON SYDNEY AUCKLAND

First published in Great Britain 1996 with permission from
InterVarsity Press – USA, Downers Grove, Illinois 60515.

10 9 8 7 6 5 4 3 2 1

British Library Cataloguing in Publication Data
A record for this book is available from the British Library

ISBN 0 340 66141 0

Printed and bound in Great Britain by
Cox & Wyman, Reading, Berks.

Hodder and Stoughton Ltd
A Division of Hodder Headline PLC
338 Euston Road
London NW1 3BH

To Mike and Jason,
my 'two best guys',
for their unfailing love and support,
to the men and women who share their stories,
and to Zig Ziglar,
who inspired me to begin
witnessing in the first place

Contents

Preface

This book is not meant to be the definitive work on personality profiles, behavioural studies or theological doctrine. Rather, it shows how to be a better witness by applying the concept of four basic personality styles. *Cringe-Free Evangelism* is for Christians who want to understand more about their idiosyncrasies and those of the people around them. The better we understand who we are and why we all act the way we do, the more effectively we can communicate to people the grace of Jesus Christ.

The ideas in this book come from working for ten years in a service business where one-to-one communication skills are critical. To form a well-rounded picture of personality styles, I've also included stories from the Bible and from laypeople who regularly witness. Some examples, particularly ones focusing on personality weaknesses, might touch sensitive areas. Other stories will make you laugh aloud as you recognise in them traits of your spouse, children or friends.

Please keep in mind as you read that these stories and lists of personality traits are not meant as *facts* but as *tendencies*. They are a mere guideline to help you to examine yourself and others and to understand differences in personalities so that you can more confidently and competently act on Christ's behalf. As Keith Green's song 'Jesus Commands Us to Go' reminds us, it should be the exception if we stay behind while others witness.

1

The Personality Milkshake

My interest in personality profiles dates back to my school years. While sitting on the lawn eating lunch with two friends, I noticed a large circle of students. The centre of attention was Gina, a tall, pretty brunette who was always surrounded by a crowd of teenagers. Looking at her, I wondered if I could ever be as popular if my family were to move to another area and I made new friends. I'm not sure it was wanting to be more popular so much as genuinely questioning what makes some kids popular and others not.

In the intervening years I've had plenty of opportunity to make friends in new places. During my stint as a navy journalist, I started out a stranger at four different duty stations. Later, as civilian newlyweds, my husband and I left our roots to buy a house, start a family and build a business thousands of miles from our family and friends. After all my moves I've thought back to that fresh-start theory from school and weighed its validity. No matter how outgoing, kind and neighbourly I tried to be, I have always been as popular (or unpopular, depending on how you look at it) as I was then. My unscientific conclusion is that I am who I am.

Only a few years later did I begin to understand why.

During my early years as a self-employed portrait photographer, I soon realised that if I was going to meet my customers' needs, I had to learn their personality quirks. Worse, if I couldn't communicate with them well enough to satisfy them and sell my portraits, I would continue struggling to make sales, lose customers and eventually become a small-business failure statistic.

What does this have to do with sharing your faith in Jesus Christ? I spotted a problem in my business relationships that we all have in witnessing relationships: failing to communicate effectively results in continued struggling and fewer people who will hear and embrace the truth of Jesus Christ.

Effective communication is a process that begins by understanding your own personality quirks. You then learn to recognise the core personality of your listener. Finally, you adapt your message to fit the two personality styles.

Cringe-Free Evangelism explores this process of effective communication. It begins with a brief background on how personality profiles emerged, some guidelines on how to interpret and use them, and specific details about the four personality styles. The middle section explains how to tailor your witness to a particular personality. In the final chapters I suggest ways to begin witnessing using your personality style.

You might be tempted to skip immediately to the chapters dealing with your personality. But if you seriously intend to establish good rapport and begin communicating the gospel to others, it is just as important to understand them as it is to understand yourself.

Ancient and Modern

Palmistry and astrology were among the original ways to assess someone's personality. The palm reader determines personality characteristics from the skin folds of the hand while astrology interprets behaviour and events through the stars and other heavenly bodies. Both are still practised today, but modern scholars disregard both methods because the assumptions of each go against current scientific knowledge and because the predictions of both are inaccurate.

The Greek physician Hippocrates introduced the four basic personality profiles 2,300 years ago, naming them choleric, sanguine, phlegmatic and melancholic. About AD 200 Galen, another Greek physician, came up with a detailed list of strengths and weaknesses for the four temperaments.

Since then, students of human behaviour have written volumes of research on personality theory and books about profiles for personal and professional use. Among them are *Spirit-Controlled Temperament* by Tim LaHaye, *Personality Plus* and *Your Personality Tree* by Florence Littauer, *The Money Makeover* by Rosemarie Patterson and *Relationship Selling* by Jim Cathcart.

The two most popular systems for identifying and explaining personality differences are the Personal Profile System by Performax Systems International and the Myers-Briggs Type Indicator. Like Hippocrates, Performax explains personality types in four divisions: Dominant Director, Interactive Influencer, Steady Relater and Cautious Thinker (together they are referred to as DISC).

The Myers-Briggs system further divides the four profiles into sixteen distinct temperaments. For example, Performax would say a person is either an introvert or an extrovert (Dominant Director 'D' Choleric, or Interactive Influencer 'I' Sanguine). Myers-Briggs, however, offers eight variations for extroverts (ESTP, ESFP, ENFP, ENTP, ESTJ, ESFJ, ENFJ and ENTJ) and another eight for introverts (ISTJ, ISFJ, INFJ, INTJ, ISTP, ISFP, INFP and INTP). The letters stand for introvert, extrovert, thinker, feeler, judger, perceiver, sensor and intuitive. (Those who have explored the Myers-Briggs system will know how this list of letters relates to the basic four, but it looks like a confusing jumble to the rest of us!

Although offering only four personality styles may seem too simplistic to Myers-Briggs enthusiasts, this book concentrates on Hippocrates' basic four because I believe they are easier to explain, easier to learn and easier to use.

As we explore these four styles, be aware of the subtle differences between *personality, temperament* and *character*. Although these words are often used interchangeably, Tim LaHaye defines them separately in *Spirit-Controlled Temperament*. *Temperament*, he says, is a combination of hereditary traits that subconsciously affect our behaviour. *Character*, the 'civilised temperament', is the inborn temperament modified by upbringing, schooling, religious morals, beliefs, principles and motivations. *Personality* is the outward expression of self. It may or may not match your character, but this is the person that the world sees.

Some people object to being neatly categorised or 'spelt out', feeling that it somehow diminishes them. But looking at yourself inside should be no different from looking at your features in a mirror. Your reflection helps you enhance, not alter, the physical traits peering back at you. Your personality profile can serve as an internal mirror. When you look inside and really see your strengths and weaknesses, you will know what needs adjusting.

The strengths and weaknesses of your personality prevail by choice. Viktor Frankl, the internationally renowned psychiatrist who endured years in Nazi death camps, called our response to life's challenges 'the last of the human freedoms'. You may feel you need superhuman strength to break the unpleasant patterns in your life, and divine strength *is* available to you through prayer. But you must exercise that freedom to choose to change.

While you may benefit personally from studying personality styles, your primary goal should be learning to empathise with others. As you practise seeing situations from other people's points of view, you begin to realise that your spouse and your boss aren't out to get you; they are just responding to life in the only way they know how.

A Few Cautions

When it comes to analysing a personality, remember first of all that the various traits are *tendencies* only. These tendencies are based on preferences. Without any conscious effort, I use my right hand to scribble my name rapidly at the bottom of cards, letters, notes and cheques. It may be barely legible, but it is my legal signature. If I were to switch the pen to my left hand, I could, of course, still sign my name, though it would take more time and effort. Simply put, I *prefer* to use my right hand, but with careful, conscious thought I can use my left. The same is true of exercising familiar and unfamiliar personality traits.

Second, when you see something about yourself that you don't like, your first reaction may be to deny it. If you have trouble being objective about yourself, ask your friend or mate to help; it doesn't take a Ph.D. in psychology to observe someone else's idiosyncrasies, especially since they recur in various areas. If someone is fussy and crabby in one situation, he or she will probably be fussy and crabby in another. If fussiness is a part of your personality profile, then you have an explanation of why you act the way you do. Don't confuse an *explanation* with an *excuse*!

Consider also the *relativity factor*. Two people might be outgoing but at decidedly different levels. For example, I am an outspoken person when compared to most of the people around me. However, if you were to compare my personality to one of my ultra-outspoken friends, I would look quiet. On the other hand, I would seem a real exhibitionist next to two soft-spoken personalities. And while the world will always view both of them as quiet and reserved, side by side one will inevitably prove more outgoing.

Another factor to take into account is your *learned behaviour*. While scientists generally agree that your core personality is as unchanging as your eye colour, environment may also modify your personality development. If you are an outspoken, direct person but are continually hushed and labelled bossy as a child, you won't be as outspoken or as direct as you might have been. When you are in a situation where these traits are appreciated, however, you will rise to the occasion and blossom.

In addition, while you cannot change the basics of who you are, you can *temper your temperament*. When I first began wondering why those teenagers were more popular, I tried to be more outgoing, more gracious and more hospitable. My core personality didn't change and hasn't changed. Even after all these years of consciously working at it, I still must make a *conscious* effort. That, of course, is the key difference. You know you are acting within your true personality when what you do simply feels natural.

My final caution is to *expect objections*. Once you see that personality profiles can be valuable, you may analyse everyone you meet. Some people will think your findings are fun and insightful; others will be offended. The biggest criticisms you'll hear are that the four personalities are too few and too limiting, too theoretical and too abstract, too unscientific, too intuitive and too infringing on privacy. When I meet someone who really objects to the personality-profile concept, I simply don't mention it again.

If you heed these warnings, appreciate that the system isn't perfect, and don't try to open a family-therapy clinic based on this book, you will be better able to interpret the observations you've already been making about the people around you.

Appreciating Uniqueness

As you read the following examples, don't feel that it's a case of the introverts versus the extroverts, or the good personality versus the bad. Each personality is a unique blend. You will find that you have one main personality style, with a secondary one following close behind. Author Tim LaHaye calls these 'personality blends'. You will also notice bits and pieces of the other two personality styles in your daily activities, but they won't feel as natural or as easily expressed as your dominant styles.

No single personality style is better than another. According to Genesis 1, after God created heaven and earth and made humans in his image, he declared that 'it was very good'. I like to look at the strength of each personality as gifts from God. When Christians work together as a team and truly appreciate the special blessings of each personality, we are presenting to the world a more accurate picture of the goodness of God the Father. When we witness by first identifying that piece of God within the person in front of us, we are respecting and appreciating the good of God's creation. We also take a giant step towards building a connection between two human beings, which could eventually be the love and the knowledge of God within them both.

The Four Personality Styles

The director choleric is motivated by a desire for power and prestige. The motto of this outgoing personality is 'Be the Best.' The director is always busy, gets right to the point in conversations, wants immediate results, thrives on power and risk-taking, works well independently and tends to concentrate on the positive in life. On the down side, the director can be a workaholic with few friends – bossy, overbearing, more concerned with a task than with the people involved.

The entertainer sanguine is motivated by the desire to have fun and to be loved by all people. This outgoing person's motto is 'Be Happy!' The entertainer is the life and soul of the party, the office and the home because he or she brings sparkle, laughter and fun. In addition to wanting to be surrounded by people, they work well with a flexible schedule where they can make spontaneous decisions. But the entertainer can talk too much, have trouble finishing projects and appear too silly to be trusted with a serious task.

The peacekeeper phlegmatic is the quiet, calming influence who keeps everyone happily and smoothly working together. The peacekeeper is friendly, likeable, soft-spoken, slow to anger and happy to stay with a job that others have long since become bored with. The motto of the peacekeeper is 'Be Pleasant.' This gentle soul can be too passive, too slow to make decisions, too afraid to voice an opinion and too quick to compromise.

The analyser melancholic pushes for perfection, and he or

she thrives on facts and details. This quiet personality works best independently, is very neat and organised, is a stickler for punctuality and has the motto 'Be Correct.' The analyser can be too critical, too pessimistic and too concerned with weighing all the facts before finally (if ever) making a decision.

You will notice all of the personalities have strengths that, when pushed to excess, become weaknesses. It is those weaknesses that make most of us wish we were another personality. Although we can try to change, remember: our core personality is about as set as the colour of our eyes. Fortunately, we are not called to be anybody but ourselves. We are no different from Jeremiah, whom God spoke to saying, 'Before I formed you in the womb I knew you, before you were born I set you apart' (Jer. 1:5).

If you don't recognise yourself in the above vignettes, or if you want an easy way to spot the core personality of others, take the following simple test.

Personality-Profile Quiz

Is your observable behaviour typically outgoing or reserved?

Outgoing

1. Are you interested more in interacting with others or in being the boss?

   Interact = Entertainer

   Boss = Director

2. If you are interested in both, are you more concerned with people liking you or with completing the job in hand?

   People = Entertainer

   Job = Director

Reserved

1. Are you more interested in making sure people are happily working together or in getting the job done correctly?

People = Peacekeeper
Job = Analyser

2. If you are interested in both, do you generally accept others at face value, or do you usually make a gut-level judgment about them?

Accept = Peacekeeper
Judge = Analyser

The Perfect Team

The more you study personality profiles, the more it becomes obvious that we all need each other. For example, the perfect team needs the director to get things organised, the entertainer to keep the mood light, the peacekeeper for stability and harmony and the analyser to work out the details. A group of four directors would fight over who was in charge; four entertainers would have a good time but never get round to working on the project; four peacekeepers would never decide who was to do what so the task would never get started; and four analysers would keep reading the bylaws or instruction manual until every issue had been analysed to shreds!

Not only are balanced teams ideal in the work place, but they also balance out our personal lives. 'Opposites attract' is not just an old saying. It is very common for spouses to be from opposite sides of the personality-profile spectrum. (Of course, the irony is that the traits we were attracted to in courtship are the very things that annoy us in marriage.) I am an outspoken director and my husband, Mike, is a reserved analyser. Nearly all of my closest female friends are quiet peacekeepers who are married to the ultimate entertainers, who are ideal friends for Mike.

When we get a foursome together for a special activity,

we really have a well-balanced team. For example, when we pack up our camping gear and head for the mountains with Lynn and Peter, we each naturally fall into the jobs defined by our personality milkshake. I use my director skills and take charge of management details, such as making a meal plan, organising a joint grocery list, overseeing packing the car and getting the receipt handy from the advance booking I made months before. Meanwhile Lynn, the entertainer, will flit from job to job spreading peace and goodwill, stop to chat with the neighbours, play with the baby and generally make the rest of us wonder if she is planning to go camping this weekend or next. (Of course, she does make the rest of us lighten up, so it is really hard to get annoyed at her when she gets sidetracked.) Her peacekeeper husband, Peter, will work steadily, lugging camping gear down from the attic and out to the car. Mike, the detail-minded analyser, meticulously checks each piece of equipment, making sure the gas cylinders are full, the tent-poles and groundsheet are included in the tent bag, the vehicle is tuned up and our route is carefully planned.

Personality match-ups are also evident throughout the Bible. The dominant director Paul was tempered by the reserved analyser Timothy. When the cautiousness trait of analyser Moses came out, God let the confident public-speaking skills of entertainer brother Aaron do the talking to move the Israelites out of Egypt.

Again, each personality has positive traits, and a personality profile fails if it makes you feel bad. You need to find your balance point by focusing on the good traits while making a conscious effort to rein your weaknesses. Use the examples in the following chapters as a guideline. Since we spend most of our time outside church walls, the examples in the next four chapters include a variety of scenarios to help you recognise each of the personalities at home, work, school, play and church. I encourage you to jot down your strengths and weaknesses as you read. This will help you put the pieces together when you're reading the later chapters on how to use your personality to be a better witness.

A note on sources: whenever possible, I credit the sources for the anecdotes and examples you'll read. Unfortunately, some of the stories and quotes come from my diary, where I seldom documented sources because I had no idea I would someday write a book on this topic. If you are interested in learning more about some aspect of personality types, look at the bibliography, where I've listed a number of informative books.

When you understand your unique blend of personality traits, you will begin to see the contributions you can make to the world around you through your work, personal relationships, Christian service and witnessing. Instead of wishing you could be more like someone else, you will learn to use your special traits for the ultimate purpose God has for you. As Thomas Aquinas said, 'God made everything, including man, for a purpose. The highest good of all things is the realisation of this purpose. As man realises this purpose, he reveals God's goodness. The highest good is the realisation of oneself as God has ordained.'

So instead of trying to come up with reasons why we think we are not what our personality-profile lists say we are, we should celebrate the good things and thank God for our particular gifts. As you discover and use these personality strengths to tell others God's message of salvation, you can tell it in a way that is right for you.

Personality Chart

Director	Entertainer	Peacekeeper	Analyser
Nature			
Assertive Extrovert	Bubbly Extrovert	Gentle Introvert	Reserved Introvert
Clothing			
Businesslike	Fashionable	Comfortable	Conservative
Conversation			
Confident, direct, at ease with large groups	Loud, funny, at ease with large groups	Quiet, low-key, prefers small groups	Slow, thoughtful, prefers small groups
Gestures			
Points for emphasis	Gestures expressively	Puts hands behind back	Puts hands in pockets
Pace			
Fast/decisive	Fast/spontaneous	Slow/easygoing	Slow/systematic
Top Priority			
Success	Popularity	Relationships	Perfection
Attitude			
Optimistic	Excitable	Peaceful	Pessimistic
Dislikes			
Incompetence, slow decision-making	9 to 5 routine, rigid rules	Abruptness, insensitivity	Surprises, changes in routine
Fears			
Loss of authority	Social rejection	Confrontation	Embarrassment
Response Under Pressure			
Dictation	Sarcasm	Silence	Withdrawal

Director	Entertainer	Peacekeeper	Analyser
Work Strengths			
Born leader; confident, organised	Good speaker; enthusiastic, energetic	Good mediator; loyal, consistent	Born thinker; meticulous, thorough
Work Weaknesses			
Abrupt, bossy	Disorganised, distracted	Dilatory, slow to adjust to change	Inflexible, compulsive over details
Decision Requirements			
Details on outcome or benefit	Definite personal benefit	Guarantee of low risk	Precise facts and figures
Decisions			
Definite	Spontaneous	Slow, but final	Well-researched
Attitude About Personal Goals			
Keeps a mental list	Has trouble deciding which to set	Puts off making	Waits for perfect plan before writing down
Relationship Strengths			
Requires few friends Initiates contact Organises activities	Loves people Initiates fun Tells great stories	Gets along with others Listens well Expresses genuine compassion	Remains devoted Solves problems Offers support whenever needed
Relationship Weaknesses			
Dominates relationship Makes decisions for others Tends to be too independent	Talks too much Wants continual attention Worries too much about what peers think and say	Waits for others to call/make plans Dampens enthusiasm Avoids talking about relational conflicts	Holds grudges Avoids social situations Withholds affection

The Personality Milkshake

Director	Entertainer	Peacekeeper	Analyser
Emotional Strengths			
Strong-willed, dedicated	Charming	Unshakeably calm	Philosophical, thoughtful
Confident, self-sufficient	Humorous	Easygoing, likeable	Conscientious, sensitive
Cool under pressure	Energetic	Dependable, patient	Idealistic
Emotional Weaknesses			
Bossy	Brassy, boisterous	Stubborn	Moody, depressed
Impatient, quick-tempered	Given to mood swings	Stingy/selfish	Insecure
Inflexible, uncomplimentary	Overdramatic	Passive	Negative
Personal Motto			
Be the Best	Be Happy	Be Pleasant	Be Correct

Adapted and used by permission from Dare to Dream *by Florence Littauer (Waco, Tex.: Word, 1991). Some ideas also adapted from* Relationship Selling *by Jim Cathcart (New York: Putnam, 1990).*

2

The Director

Robert Browning must have had the highly motivated director in mind when he wrote, 'A man's reach must exceed his grasp or what's a heaven for?' This dynamic personality will overcome just about any obstacle to complete an objective. The director will use a logical approach to tackle difficult tasks and thrives on freedom, independence, variety and challenge. The fastest way to get a job completed is to tell a director it *can't* be done. He will then happily rise to the occasion just to prove you wrong!

A director will quickly dominate any new group or organisation he or she joins. One director started attending a new church in October, officially joined in December and began teaching the adult Sunday-school class and leading the youth group in January. It sounds pretty pushy as I write these words about myself, but it seemed perfectly natural at the time to take over two jobs that no one else wanted. Yet I didn't know names, had never taught a Sunday-school class, had no teaching curriculum and wasn't familiar with the church's layout (even the heating and light switches). In true director style, I acted first and handled the problems later.

The front pages of newspapers worldwide are covered with stories about this hardworking leadership figure who is typically very successful in business and politics. The

Bible also has its share. Take director Lydia (Acts 16:14). This seller of purple cloth was a successful businesswoman in an age when men were merchants and women stayed at home. This self-confident director also welcomed into her home the first Christians, part of the new radical movement, in spite of any repercussions she might have felt in her business dealings. The reason was simple: it was the right thing to do. And a director always has the confidence to stand true to values and beliefs regardless of any prospect of ridicule. Where any other personality might melt under peer pressure, the director will stand firm.

Boaz, a wealthy distant relative of Naomi and Ruth, also stood by what he believed was right when he married Ruth (Ruth 4). In spite of the censure he would feel if he (a Jew) took a foreigner as his wife, director Boaz chose to honour his family obligations by caring for Naomi and Ruth this way.

The steadfast zeal of Stephen, the first Christian martyr, is another example of a director holding his ground regardless of the consequences. Stephen could not sit quietly by, indifferent and apathetic, while Christ was being maligned. Stephen spontaneously, confidently and courageously put his life on the line for his Saviour.

Problems the rest of the world would collapse under almost inspire a director to take on the task and conquer the challenge. Elijah, the stout-hearted and thunder-voiced prophet of the Lord, was up against horrible odds, including social scorn, loneliness and murderous adversaries (1 Kings 19). He feared for his life and got depressed at times, but he persevered and remained an upright prophet, acting and speaking according to God's will. (Note that, just as the Lone Ranger had Tonto, so Elijah had his co-worker Elisha, a gentle-natured peacekeeper.) The inborn 'Lone Ranger' personality trait helped Elijah endure the days, even months, of loneliness.

Directors don't need a lot of friends to be happy. Since they are so confident of their own abilities, directors don't rely on the approval of others to be happy or to move ahead with a project. They would be just as pleased to stay late at the office completing a project as they would to go out to dinner with friends.

From these examples it is easy to see that the director is the right person for getting a job done quickly, efficiently and without complaint. Accomplishing goals is a daily priority for this results-oriented person, who will quickly move down a checklist of projects. The trouble is, while a director is a good administrator, this is not necessarily someone you want hanging around when you want a lazy day at home!

The Bold and Bossy

As with all of the personality profiles, the wonderful strengths of the director, when pushed to excess, quickly become weaknesses. Many of the director traits can, and do, get on other people's nerves. The high self-confidence factor alone is often annoying enough to make the other three profiles choose others for friends. Self-confident directors don't necessarily have to be arrogant to chase people away. Just the fact that they know who they are and what they can and should accomplish in life can be a stark contrast to the less organised and less motivated. This contrast often makes others feel insecure.

When we were visiting friends one Christmas a few years ago, I used a lull in one of the quiet afternoons to pound out the concluding chapter for the book I was completing.

Everyone in the house was involved in one quiet activity or another. Our hostess, a peacekeeper, was playing with her son's new video computer toy. When she realised what I was doing, she said, 'It is a good thing I have high self-esteem, or it would bother me that I'm lounging on the sofa playing a video game while Helen sits at the computer finishing her fourth book.' She didn't say it sarcastically, but the message was clear.

The core personality traits that make the director such a strong leader also become annoying bad habits when left unchecked. *Bossiness* heads the list. Since directors care more about getting the job done than keeping people happy along the way, they trample a few people along the road to completion. It isn't so much that directors intend to be mean, but they know they can work faster and more efficiently without all these other people slowing things down. The director can be impatient, too direct, too abrupt, too quick-tempered, too inflexible and too intolerant of mistakes. Instead of slowing the pace so others can keep up, a director opens the gears and blasts ahead, disregarding everyone's thoughts and feelings. When these energetic extroverts act first and think later, rash words and actions will inevitably catch up with them. Then, to annoy the other personalities involved even more, directors always manage to rationalise their actions and place the blame on someone else.

Practicality is another key trait of the director. It has a complimentary ring to it, but practicality can be annoying even to directors themselves, who get tired of being realistic. Being practical is sometimes like having your own built-in killjoy. I could tell you many stories of how some of my fabulous plans were stillborn because of my practical nature, but I will limit it to two.

When I was in my early teens, we lived just one street

away from my bosom friend, Sherry. We alternated between the two houses, depending on who was feuding with her parents. We usually started at Sherry's, but she inevitably got furious with her mother. Sherry would slam the front door as she yelled at her mother that she was running away from home.

Whenever I was angry enough to want to leave home, I would climb the long staircase to my room, pull out my savings book and determine how long I could live on the meagre balance. It didn't take much to work out that I would ultimately run out of money and have to come crawling back. I was too practical to storm out of the door when I knew one day I would have to swallow my pride and come home.

Being too practical also took the fluff and sparkle out of my wedding gown. During the nine months between engagement ring and wedding day, I was separated from my fiancé. He was in New York, while I was stationed at a naval base eleven hundred miles away in Memphis.

With nine lonely months looming ahead, I decided I had plenty of time to make the wedding gown of my dreams – an elaborate design complete with a beaded bodice, delicate lace and a full-length train. I wanted to compare the cost of making the gown with buying one. In the process of comparing prices, I decided it would be even more practical to buy or make a dress that I could wear again – after the wedding day.

Without ever trying on a real wedding gown, I bought a floor-length dress that I could wear, and have worn, again. It was a decision I eventually regretted. Years later, as I photographed gown after lovely wedding gown, I repeatedly wished I had been less practical and more fun!

As you can see, you don't have to wait until you're an

adult to notice the strengths and weaknesses of a director. They definitely show up early. The bull-headed, outspoken, 'don't tell me what to do' extroverts are the 'terrible twos' of your worst nightmare, the toddlers who stamp their feet and demand to get their way *right now!* The director child will be the leader, organiser and initiator in his group of friends, and he will always have a plan for what he wants to be when he grows up.

The Courageous and the Corrupt

Paul is a prime example of a director. As Saul, he persecuted Christians with an unchecked vengeance. After his transformation on the road to Damascus, nothing could intimidate him into keeping quiet. Once he knew his mission was to share the good news with the Gentiles, nothing was going to stop him. He was courageous, outspoken, stubborn, faithful and indifferent to criticism. The book of Acts is an impressive list of the places Paul preached, and the volumes of letters he wrote became what author Frank S. Mead (*Who's Who in the Bible*) calls the 'superstructure, the sides and the walls' of our Christian faith.

All of these accomplishments suggest glowing personal qualities, but that was not always the case. When Paul first arrived in the Christian community, he scared them to death; after all, he was 'the man who raised havoc in Jerusalem among those who call on [Jesus's] name' (Acts 9:21). Nor did unbelievers take to him. Shortly after his conversion he spoke and debated with some Greek-speaking Jews who got so angry they tried to murder him (Acts 9:28–31). Paul had to be whisked out of the country to save his life. The very next verse gives us a clue to the relief felt when an overbearing director leaves the room: 'Then the church throughout Judea, Galilee and Samaria enjoyed a time of peace' (v. 31).

Once Paul was tempered with tolerance and humility, God was able to use him to accomplish great things. Paul writes about his new attitude in 1 Corinthians 2:1–5.

> When I came to you, brothers, I did not come with eloquence or superior wisdom as I proclaimed to you the testimony about God. For I resolved to know nothing while I was with you except Jesus Christ and him crucified. I came to you in weakness and fear, and with much trembling. My message and my preaching were not with wise and persuasive words, but with a demonstration of the Spirit's power, so that your faith might not rest on men's wisdom, but on God's power.

Only a *tempered* director could utter these words.

The same personality traits that Paul tempered, an Old Testament queen *exploited* (1 Kgs 16–21; 2 Kgs 9). The very name Jezebel stands for everything bad a woman could possibly do or be. Proud and merciless, Queen Jezebel looked down her arrogant nose at her subjects from a tower built on a four-hundred-foot hill. She had no patience with her weak, incompetent husband, so she took over for the king, writing letters in his name and signing them with his seal. Haughty to the end, she was never the slightest bit humble, contrite or sorry.

Paul and Jezebel represent the best and the worst sides of the director. Meanwhile, Miriam, the older sister of Moses, falls somewhere between them. As a child, she bravely watched Moses as he floated down the Nile in his little basket of reeds. When the Pharaoh's daughter found the infant, Miriam stepped forward and offered to find a

Hebrew woman (Moses' own mother) to nurse the baby. For a slave child to approach a princess must have taken a good deal of self-confidence and courage! Miriam showed these same traits many years later when Moses held the staff of God to part the Red Sea and she led the ex-slaves across the riverbed, dancing and singing her Song of Deliverance.

Unfortunately, that bit of glory wasn't enough to satisfy her. A year later she was discontented with her secondary role as sister to the Israelites' leader. Full of malice and envy, Miriam publicly complained about Moses. 'Has the LORD spoken only through Moses? . . . Hasn't he also spoken through [my brother Aaron and me]?' (Num. 12:2). Miriam learned two quick lessons. First, she tasted much-needed humility when God struck her with leprosy. Then she felt true grace when Moses did not revile her but begged God to cure her. Instead of enduring a life of suffering for her sins, Miriam was shut out from the camp for only seven days.

More About Negative Tendencies

We can easily point out the personality problems in other people, like Miriam and Jezebel, but it stings when it comes to our personal problems. It's wonderful that the director is independently motivated, hardworking and self-confident. But to find yourself labelled too demanding, too tactless when delegating a job and too intimidating when sharing your faith can make you cringe – and I am cringing even as I write this section.

When you read about your negative tendencies, you can't possibly hide from them (unless you flatly deny them). Personally, I can recall some school memories that still have the power to make me cringe. I remember, for example, absolutely loathing parent–teacher meetings. My friends were gleeful over the time off, but I dreaded the inevitable confrontation when my mother came home from hearing about all the bad things I had done at school. One year was particularly bad: year five, Mrs Jones's class.

I had walked to the shops with my classmate Alison. My mother was so furious from her meeting with my teacher that she couldn't wait for me to walk the mile or so home. She drove the blue and white Volkswagen to pick us up. No one said a word in the car, and that one-mile drive was the longest ride of my life. Once home, my mother opened her tightly clamped jaw and let me have it. I can still hear her voice, 'Helen, you're too bossy!' Never mind that my marks, homework, test results and participation ranked at the top of the class. All of that paled in comparison to my one personality trait that had got out of control.

That same tendency to be bossy haunts me even today. I have to make a huge effort to suppress it.

The Ideal-Witness Myth

You may assume that with a little self-discipline the confident director will be a natural when it comes to witnessing. But having self-confidence, a big mouth and lots of courage doesn't mean you will promptly apply all of this to your walk with Jesus Christ. Just as introverts cannot use their personality as an excuse *not* to witness, an outspoken extrovert isn't an automatic Billy Graham or Paul the apostle.

Instead of waiting till chapter 12 ('From One Director to Another') to tell you about my quest to find my place in answering Jesus's command to 'go into all the world and preach the good news to all creation' (Mark 16:15), I'm including part of my story here. That story is a large part of how this book came to be in your hands.

Cringe-Free Evangelism grew out of my own struggles to speak up and speak out for Christ. Andrew Carnegie once said, 'The secret of my success is that I listen to the nudges that I get in the wee, small hours of the night.' It was a slow, nagging nudge that put my Christianity, and this book, into action.

A professional photographer by trade, I began gaining popularity in the photography lecture circuit in 1989. As I faced rapt audiences of fifty to two hundred photographers, my quiet nudge told me I had a great opportunity to put in a few plugs for Christ. But every other part of my personality balked at this suggestion. I may be a self-confident extrovert, but we have fears too! Instead of jumping at the chance to serve God, I was thinking things like, *Witnessing from a secular podium is fine for the Zig Ziglars [a leading sales trainer, author, motivational speaker and unabashed proclaimer of the gospel in the US] and Norman Vincent Peales of the world, because everyone* knows *they are Christians and expects and accepts witnessing as a part of their presentations. I am just a lowly 'ordinary Christian' who has no business making waves.*

Yet I couldn't quieten the steady voice of the Holy Spirit, so I decided to write to Ziglar and ask how he witnessed during his seminars. In his prompt reply he wrote that he prays before each lecture that God will use him. That sounded easy enough! I thought, *That's not so bad. I know how to pray. I can do this.*

I immediately put the Zig Ziglar prayer plan into action. But just in case prayer wasn't enough, I had a backup plan. During a lecture I used a single index card with an overview outline written in microscopic type that I referred to once or twice during the talk to ensure I hadn't wandered off track. To help with my 'witnessing', I inserted one or two key words on the card to remind me to plug Christ.

It didn't work.

From the stage I may have looked supremely confident, but when it came to adding two or three sentences for Christ, I became a nervous wreck. During the first year my only bit of 'witnessing' was suggesting that the audience read *The Bible*. I included this in my list of 'Top Ten Things to Do' at the close of each lecture. Then I quickly bolted from the stage before anyone had a chance to lob a tomato my way. By just mentioning the Bible, I was sure I would be labelled a religious fanatic.

I was disappointed with myself for not having more courage and with God for not answering my prayers. When I sat down and analysed the series of seminars I had given with my intended plug for Christ, it didn't take long to realise that I hadn't prepared myself for God to answer my prayers. Much as a little girl dreams of Prince Charming riding up on a white horse with colours flying to rescue the princess from the clutches of the wicked witch, I expected God to do all the work.

Ziglar writes about this dilemma in his book *Confessions of a Happy Christian*. To people who complain about God not using them, he says, 'God cannot do much *through* us until he gets *in* us. The moment Christ comes in, he then proceeds to chip away the parts which don't look like a Christian.'

In retrospect I realise that I would never expect to become a better photographer without reading books, attending lectures and workshops, and putting roll after roll of film through the camera. But I expected God to let me take a short cut to sharing my faith without preparing properly. So I piled up the books and tapes and attended seminars and trained my mind to receive the message God had already given my heart. Only after I had done my part could I expect God to do his.

Whether God knocks you off a horse on the road to Damascus, strikes you with leprosy or lets you babble foolishly on stage in front of your peers, the ultimate aim is to soften that tough outer shell and teach us that we cannot do it on our own. Like Paul, we must be humble enough to accept the fact that God doesn't need us. We need him.

3

The Entertainer

On the stage of life the world's funniest, most charming, most outgoing and most optimistic people are entertainers. Like Gina, the girl I envied in school, entertainers love being the centre of attention. Where the director flatly tells people what to do to get a job done, the entertainer would much rather influence peers and subordinates so they will willingly accomplish a task.

You can easily pick out the entertainer in any environment because they are both vocal and visual. This flashy personality dresses confidently in the newest styles and colours – fashions that other personalities might feel a bit foolish wearing. At a recent weekend church retreat Lynn, an entertainer, was dressed in an old blue-plaid flannel shirt, worn untucked and unbuttoned over a T-shirt – the hottest trend among teenagers. When I asked Lynn about her outfit, she replied, 'Yes, I know this is the "in" look. I always like to keep up with what's in style with the kids.'

Another entertainer friend outdresses everyone at fancy dress parties. He once won first prize at a Hallowe'en party for coming as a six-foot-five, eighteen-stone, pink-tutu-clad ballerina. Another time he wore lime-green shorts and a Hawaiian print shirt to a country and western theme party.

If you haven't been able to find the entertainers in your life by how they dress, you can pick them out from across the room as they talk. While directors point for emphasis as they tell others what to do, entertainers use sweeping arm gestures to illustrate what they say.

I once spotted an entertainer driving a red sports car. On holiday one spring, getting away from the last winter weather of home, we were excited to see people driving with the tops on their convertibles down – until we saw that the driver ahead was looking more over his shoulder to speak to his passengers than he was looking at the cars rushing around us. We prudently slowed and let someone else slide into the danger spot.

Livening Things Up

If you listen to these hand-waving, eye-contact entertainers, you will hear witty stories about their daily activities. Told by another personality, these same stories would sound mundane. Entertainers, however, use their creative, colourful and charming wit to transform an ordinary event into an extraordinary story. These verbal skills make entertainers excellent at putting complex concepts into simple and understandable terms, and they often turn these talents to sales and public relations.

The entertainer has a zest for living. When our friend John first learned how to ski, he didn't like anything about it. His companions, however, encouraged him to stick with it: 'Just ski like you drive.' He tried it that way – full speed ahead, Geronimo John! – and he's loved it ever since.

John's entertainer exuberance comes naturally. One July afternoon when we were pulling him on waterskis behind our boat, we couldn't make the ride bumpy enough for him. As he threw body and soul into having a wild time, his wife commented, 'John puts that much energy into everything he does. Everything!'

It is easy to tell if one of your children is an entertainer. Our son Jason is a good example. Everyone has always liked Jason. Even when he was very young, he knew just what to say and do to charm his way into the hearts of all our friends. That was no small feat when you consider most of these friends had no children and weren't really comfortable with them.

Not only have people always liked Jason, he has always liked people. When he started attending playgroup, instead of getting upset like all the other children when I dropped him off, he cried when I came to pick him up. I had to make a point of arriving when only two or three other children remained. Again during primary school, when he attended the after-school club for children of working parents, he never wanted me to pick him up early. The few times I tried, he asked me to go home and come back at 5.30 when everyone else got picked up. By the time he reached secondary school he told me flat out, 'My friends are my life.'

Jason used his natural speaking talents and stage presence to land leading roles in school plays right from the start. His fashion flair and personal confidence – both traits of the true entertainer – have drawn similar attention. When Jason was in year five he wore pink high-top trainers to school one day just to see if anyone would notice. (How could they not?) And one day, when class members were encouraged to dress as a teacher, he wore a long, dowdy skirt and black heels, donned a clipboard and glasses, and paraded with the other 'teachers' in the guise of the matronly school headmistress.

Parents of an entertainer will notice early on another common trait. Unlike the upbeat, motivated director, the entertainer can quickly change moods. There is no middle ground. The day is either fabulously wonderful or dismally horrible. With personal recognition and prestige high on the list of values, this applause-seeking soul is sensitive to criticism. Emotional entertainers can burst into tears at the slightest criticism while everyone else remains clueless to what caused the outburst. Fortunately, they will just as quickly switch back to an energised, emotional high.

When the Charm Wears Off

When you take all the positive personality traits of the entertainer, you have a charming person who knows just what to say and when to say it. However, as we have been trying to teach our son for years, too much of *anything* is not good. All that charm, all that talking and all that fun and frivolity can get old. In fact, the other three personalities might feel that the entertainer is putting on a front and that he or she has no depth or soul or true concern. Personality may be an explanation for how and why entertainers, or any persons of any profile, act the way they do, but personality can never excuse a lack of connection and communication with people of other personalities.

The weaknesses of the entertainer grow out of the strengths. Obviously no one can be the centre of attention all the time, and the entertainer needs to learn to relinquish the spotlight occasionally. Instead of doing all the talking, the entertainer needs to ask questions and truly listen to answers, in the meantime resisting the urge to interject smart-alec quips. Repeating the same stories and anecdotes in minute detail is another bad habit. A considerate entertainer will consider telling new stories with less detail. Finally, some overboisterous entertainers might try speaking more softly. You know just who I mean if you have ever held the phone a foot from your ear and everyone in the room has easily heard what was said.

Other problem areas for entertainers revolve around their desire for companionship and approval. The need to be around people all the time can become emotionally unhealthy. One of our entertainer friends feels so strongly about not being alone that he will actually go back to work if he happens to come home and find his wife and children out. A powerful drive for popularity and a susceptibility to peer pressure are two other particularly challenging issues for entertainers.

Vanity can be another problem. In the film *Anne of Green Gables,* based on L. M. Montgomery's novels, the red-haired entertainer Anne breaks a slate over a boy's head because he called her Carrots. On the way home from school she buys dye from a pedlar who promises it will colour her hair brown. Desperate to improve her looks, she tries it. Her hair turns green instead!

Impetuously volunteering for committees and projects is a trait that gets the entertainer in more trouble than anything. This enthusiastic person loves to volunteer. The trouble is, once the initial pats on the back for taking on the task have subsided, the motivation to finish does too. The entertainer always intends to complete the project, but something else usually comes along that looks more interesting. Entertainers waste time talking, have their priorities out of order and quickly lose momentum.

The various teachers' comments on one of Jason's school reports are typical for an entertainer who has stepped over the line: 'Inconsistent.' 'Needs to worry more about himself and less about others.' 'I think he would do well if he would just settle down and concentrate.'

Others soon learn that entertainers start more tasks than

they finish and that they do a lot of talking along the way. Consequently, the more serious personality styles have trouble trusting this haphazard person with important work. Disorganised entertainers often don't reach their full potential because they refuse to follow through and *finish* what they start.

Everyone's true character comes out under pressure, and the charm and wit of the entertainer take on an entirely new form: sarcasm. Their jokes are no longer light. The stories are no longer funny. When under pressure the director resorts to bullying, but entertainers attempt to take the heat off themselves by sarcastically poking fun at others.

Dazzling Displays

God used entertainers in both Old and New Testament times. Peter followed Christ spontaneously, and he continued to act impulsively, jumping overboard into a raging sea, drawing a sword to protect Jesus in Gethsemane and then denying that he knew 'the king of the Jews' when a servant girl laughed at him for being a follower.

Peter's turning point came when Christ reached through his shame, forgave him and called him to use his people skills to found the Church. Peter quickly accepted Christ's gracious forgiveness and his challenge. While speaking to a crowd at Pentecost, Peter used his storytelling ability to explain Jesus in terms the people could understand. Reminding them that King David had spoken of the death and resurrection of the Messiah, Peter told them of Christ. Crowds of people responded to Peter's warmhearted nature and his message. 'When the people heard [of Jesus's crucifixion], they were cut to the heart . . . Those who accepted his message were baptised, and about three thousand were added to their number that day' (Acts 2:37, 41).

Aaron, the entertainer God used as the spokesperson and aide to Moses, used his communication skills and outgoing personality to unify the Israelites and relate God's messages to Pharaoh. Although he eagerly answered God's call to serve, Aaron cracked under peer pressure. When the Israelites pressed him for a god to worship when Moses was gone on the mountain, Aaron erected a golden calf. Then he sidestepped responsibility and let Miriam take the blame for the rebellion they had foolishly planned together. Ultimately Aaron died in disgrace, stripped of his priestly robes and position.

Samson, the Hercules of the Bible, is another example of an impetuous entertainer. His birth was predicted by an angel, and he was consecrated as a Nazirite, a special servant of God from the moment of his birth until his death. His hair – the symbol of his dedication to God and his strength – was never to be cut. God designated Samson to save his people from the Philistines, and Samson did it with the colourful flair of an entertainer. For example, he killed a lion with his bare hands, slaughtered a thousand Philistines with the jawbone of an ass, and tied three hundred foxes together in pairs with a lighted torch between and let them loose in Philistine fields.

Vanity was Samson's downfall. He told a pretty woman the secret of his strength, and the Philistines paid for the knowledge. They shaved his head, blinded him and bound his wrists and ankles. But God didn't give up on the imprisoned Samson, and Samson didn't lose his faith in God. As his humility grew, so did his hair. While a crowd of three thousand Philistines mocked the blind, chained prisoner during a temple celebration to their god Dagon, Samson prayed for a chance to redeem himself. With renewed faith and renewed strength, he pushed over a huge support pillar and caused more Philistines to tumble to their deaths in one moment than all he had killed during his entire lifetime.

King David was an entertainer with both good days and bad. As the youngest son, he spent his youth quietly watching the family sheep at remote pastures. Even after he killed Goliath, he went back to quietly tending sheep. But when God thrust David into the limelight by anointing him king of Israel, the true entertainer emerged. With close personal relationships continuing to be a priority, entertainer David remained true to King Saul and his heir apparent, Jonathan. David set his friendships with Saul and Jonathan above even Saul's death threats, choosing not to slay Saul even when he had more than one opportunity.

After the Philistines killed Saul and David truly became king, the fearless warrior ruled his people with love. He was a poet and a musician, and he danced joyfully in the streets to express his love for God. When David's love for God grew weaker than his love of self, however, he became an adulterer and a murderer. But David turned his penitent heart back to God, and God honoured him by allowing Jesus to be born of the 'house and line of David' (Luke 2:4).

Speaking Up

Though we may sometimes envy entertainers' ability to attract people and power, the above profiles illustrate how entertainers can lean heavily on their strengths – charm, magnetism, communication skills – and turn them into weaknesses. Clearly the entertainer does not automatically put together just the right mix of strengths.

Although the quiet types might want to leave the faith-sharing command to this outgoing, talkative, personable profile, it is unfair to expect witnessing to come any more naturally to entertainers than it does to the other three-quarters of the population. The fact that someone is an extrovert doesn't mean that witnessing will be easy for him or her. After all, how can we expect the very personality who desperately needs acceptance by peers to readily become a zealous, door-knocking evangelist? Since entertainers' greatest vulnerability is fear of rejection, of course they will hesitate before they open their mouths and put their lives/values/souls on the line for Christ.

Being an entertainer is not an excuse *not* to witness, nor is it a special reason *to* witness. Like the other personalities, playful, stimulating entertainers simply need to come to terms with their strengths and weaknesses and discover how to 'package' themselves for Christ.

4

The Peacekeeper

The peacekeeper – easygoing, patient, responsible, hard-working and dependable – is the person everyone loves to have around. Part of the low profile includes dressing in casual clothing that blends in with everyone else, and the less bother the better.

Maintaining close personal relationships with friends, family members and co-workers is the number one priority of this soft-spoken, steady type. More than anything else, peacekeepers fear confrontation in relationships, and they will give in under pressure to avoid an outright fight or argument.

Amie, one of the most gracious women I know, calls this the 'doormat mode'. She lives with her husband and two small children in a big house overlooking a quiet pond in the country. The beautiful setting comes complete with a revolving front door and a steady stream of guests all summer long; every weekend from May to September is booked up with friends, friends of friends, relatives and friends of relatives. When I asked Amie about it, she said, 'I've been a doormat for my family all my life. I just can't say no!'

Saying yes is perfectly in harmony with this generous soul's primary reason for living: keeping the peace and smoothing out the rough spots on the rest of us. The peacekeeper may have a hard time getting started on a project, but once started will happily see it through to completion. This loyal, pleasant person co-operates well with others, is a good listener and is content to continue working on a job long after the other personalities have become bored. With a peacekeeper on your committee, you can be guaranteed stability for many years to come.

The Bible is full of glowing stories of peacekeepers.

Abigail used her humble nature and mediator skills to soothe David when her drunken husband refused to offer hospitality to the future king. Without her sincere apology and gifts of food and drink to the band of six hundred men, the infuriated David would have made Abigail's husband pay for his insults (1 Sam. 25).

Only a peacekeeper like Job could accept the suffering heaped on him as the test of faith it was. Any other personality would have been belligerent and bitter when Satan killed his family, burned his home and raided his livestock. After all this, Job fell down on the ground before God and said, 'Naked I came from my mother's womb, and naked I shall depart. The LORD gave and the LORD has taken away; may the name of the LORD be praised' (Job 1:21). Job's faith remained firm, and only a painful illness and the critical remarks of friends caused him finally to sin by demanding of God, 'Let the Almighty answer *me*' (Job 31:35). In the end he repented of even that, and God restored his prosperity.

Ruth was also a gentle peacekeeper. When Naomi's sons died and she told her two daughters-in-law to return to their own people, Ruth said, 'Don't urge me to leave you or to turn back from you. Where you go I will go, and where you stay I will stay. Your people will be my people and your God my God' (Ruth 1:16). Ruth gave up her country, friends, family and the chance to marry a man of her own nationality because of her singular devotion to Naomi. In true peacekeeper style, she firmly made up her mind, and there was no changing it.

The apostle John, greatly loved by Jesus, didn't seem to get involved in the bickering and pettiness of the other disciples. He described for us in the book of Revelation the wonders he envisioned while alone on the island of Patmos.

Another peacekeeper who quietly left her legacy to the world was Mary, the mother of Jesus. She was a humble, obscure peasant girl who never wore fancy clothes and never sought personal glory. When the angel told her of her forthcoming pregnancy, she graciously accepted the news, saying, 'I am the Lord's servant . . . May it be to me as you have said' (Luke 1:38). After the miraculous evidences of God's work at the birth of Jesus, she 'treasured up all these things and pondered them in her heart' (Luke 2:19). The abrupt, logical director would have challenged the angel to a duel of wits, while the talkative egotistical entertainer would have blasted the news from one end of the Roman Empire to the other.

From Peaceful to Passive

With all these wonderful accounts of biblical peacekeepers, it is hard to imagine that this quiet, watchful, compassionate person has any faults. However, just as the director's leadership can turn to bossiness and the entertainer's charm to sarcasm, the peacekeeper's concern can become pushiness – bad news for those of us who don't want all of our wrinkles smoothed out.

A peacekeeper friend tried to correct my lack of interest in politics by giving a donation in my name and signing me up to receive monthly mailings from a political action group that informs subscribers what issues are being debated in government. The mailing comes complete with what to say and where to write to support the organisation's stand. Her method worked on one point but failed on another. I realised I did have a strong point of view on political issues; it just didn't match hers. Every month I tossed the unopened circular in the bin.

Since peacekeepers don't often show extremes in expression, they can be accused of being unfeeling, unresponsive and unenthusiastic to people close to them. The worst-case scenario is a human being with little more personality than a piece of furniture. As an extension of not being naturally outgoing and giving, peacekeepers give the lowest tips and the least expensive gifts. At times they can be downright stingy.

When pushed to the extreme, the steadiness that makes the peacekeeper so good at smoothing out the rough edges of life can become procrastination. A writer friend preferred pecking away on her manual typewriter an extra decade before finally giving in and buying a computer. She waited about the same length of time before finally deciding a microwave oven was safe to use in her home.

Also, since it takes so long for peacekeepers to make decisions, they tend to freeze up if any last-minute changes need to be made. Their slow pace can be infuriating to the faster-moving directors and entertainers, who often think peacekeepers are being lazy and deliberately resisting much-needed change. The outspoken personalities will also be annoyed that the peacekeeper continually creates ripples of realism on the director's 'brilliant' plans and the entertainer's 'carefree' ideas.

When peacekeepers finally make a decision, they can be too stubborn about sticking with it. One day I photographed a young family at the mother's request. When the time came to select the favourite pose to make into the completed portraits, the entertainer mother could not get her peacekeeper husband to agree on anything other than that he liked the photographs. Two weeks later he announced he wanted a divorce. No discussion. No comment. After fifteen years, their marriage was suddenly at an end.

Walking away from a marriage is an extreme response, but it is not as rare as one might think. When I used this story to illustrate peacekeeper extremes at a recent photography workshop, a Vermont photographer told me later, 'I can't believe it. You just described the last year and a half of my life. My wife got up out of bed at three in the morning and left me. I've been trying for a year and a half to get her to talk about why she left and how we can get back together, and she won't discuss it. No matter what I say or do, she won't budge.'

This type of behaviour makes sense when you understand the peacekeeper's thought process. Peacekeepers will do anything to avoid their number one fear – controversy. They don't want to fight, so they don't voice objections. Instead they hold all their unhappiness inside. When they can't stand it any more they walk away. After suppressing their unhappiness for so long, they will not easily or willingly listen to the other side of the issue.

Amazing as it sounds, it is also possible to be overconcerned about others. Peacekeepers can be so concerned about not hurting someone's feelings that they don't make the right decision or take the right action. Since this co-operative person desperately wants to avoid confrontation, he or she will do anything to keep from making a decision that could upset someone. Being so sensitive to the feelings and needs of others can also leave the peacekeeper open to being unduly influenced or manipulated.

You can see these strengths and weaknesses in your peacekeeper child. Everyone likes this quiet, easygoing child because she or he will never deliberately do anything wrong. Peacekeepers don't want to draw attention to themselves or get into trouble of any kind. One father recently lamented, 'I wish our teenage daughter would do some little thing wrong once in a while. She just doesn't seem "normal"!'

Faster-paced parents will probably become frustrated with having an introvert in the house who never initiates phone calls to friends, goes outside to play only when prodded and seems to spend too much time alone. Peacekeeper children rarely get involved in extracurricular activities at school, and they have trouble deciding on what they want to be when they grow up. It is not that they don't have friends or interests; they just feel that making decisions and finalising plans is too much trouble. For this reason, perhaps, once peacekeepers decide on professions, absolutely nothing will change their minds.

An Array of Biblical Peacekeepers

Abraham was most likely a soft-spoken peacekeeper because of how he handled stress and strife. To avoid confrontation with the Egyptians, he asked his wife to pretend she was his sister. His peacekeeper mode also came into play when his tribe and Lot's were bickering over pasture land (Gen. 13). To avoid conflict Abraham let Lot have first choice over all the land, settling for whatever was left. Later, acting on staunch loyalty to family, he interceded for Lot when the Lord God was going to destroy Sodom. When God tested him by asking him to give up his son, Abraham proved loyal to Jehovah. Because of Abraham's steadfast faith, dependable nature and devotion, God blessed him, and he became the father of a mighty nation.

The dilemma of devotion also struck Jonathan, Saul's son. Loving David as his brother, he pleaded for David's life when Saul passed an edict for his death. When Saul would show no mercy, Jonathan sneaked out to warn his friend. Jonathan was loyal to his father to the end, but his heart was with David.

Stuck in a harem for a heartless king, peacekeeper Esther was caught in a no-win situation: either she would be a one-night stand and then a permanent outcast from her people, the Jews, or she would be queen of the country that held Jews in slavery. She followed the advice of her cousin Mordecai about not telling anyone she was Jewish, although that meant she could not live a kosher life. She also passively followed instructions on how to dress for her big night with the king, who was ultimately delighted and crowned her his queen. When trouble for the Jews arose because of Haman, the king's right-hand man, Esther, seeking to avoid conflict, ignored her obligation to speak up for her people. Finally Mordecai pointed out that God would punish her whether she was 'safe' inside the castle walls or outside with her people. She replied, 'I will go to the king, even though it is against the law. And if I perish, I perish' (Esther 4:16). Having made her decision, she laid a plan that showed great insight. Her intercession saved the Jews from a cruel slaughter.

Jesus praised Mary, the sister of Martha, for sitting at his feet and listening attentively to his teachings. He also praised her devotion when she poured a costly bottle of oil on his feet. Meanwhile, Martha could not help but be annoyed that her passive little sister had found a convenient way to get out of work.

Eli, the high priest who ruled at Shiloh between the era of the judges and that of the kings, was a peacekeeper too timid to stand up for his beliefs. Although he loved the Lord and the ark of God, he was too spineless to stand up to his own sons, who abused their priestly robes and defiled God's house. God warned Eli that he would kill them, but Eli still could not confront his sons.

Opposites Attract

God seems to balance out our strengths and weaknesses by attracting us to friends and spouses who complement our shortcomings. Eli had industrious Samuel, Mary had Martha, Abraham had Sarah, Naomi had Ruth, and Esther had Mordecai. As God made matches with the people of the Bible, so he does with us today. Nearly all of my close friends are peacekeepers. As a director/entertainer, I am attracted to the gentle nature and the slow and easy pace of peacekeepers. They inevitably help me out of personal or business scrapes of one kind or another.

As a family and children portrait photographer, I attract a particularly large number of peacekeepers as clients. When a customer has a problem, I tend to automatically overreact, so I phone peacekeeper Brenda, a fellow photographer. Her pleasant, relaxed voice always calms me down. She inevitably offers a peaceful way to *respond* (not react) to the problem at hand. When I told her how much I appreciate and envy her ability to respond sensitively and patiently to crises, she said, 'Just once I would like to scream and yell, slam down the telephone receiver and storm out of the door!' I must confess, it was reassuring to know that while I would do anything to have her tranquil nature, she longs to be a bit more bold.

My school chum Tootie is also a peacekeeper. During a recent visit to my home town, I was determined not to be my usual bossy self. Tootie and I had several free days together, and I thought it was high time I let her choose the activities. The first day the conversation went something like this:

'What do you want to do, Tootie?'

'I don't really care, Helen. Whatever you want to do is fine.'

After a day of hanging around, I put my organisation hat back on. The next day we went to a shopping centre in the morning, met some school friends for lunch, took our sons to an aircraft museum, visited her mother and went swimming.

When I explained my little experiment to Tootie, she said she didn't mind that I planned everything. Since no one objected to the busy agenda, I kept the pace lively for the rest of my visit.

Along the same lines, a woman told me about her annual grand shopping trip with her two sisters. She said her husband has fussed at her for years about how the two older sisters, both peacekeepers, were bossed around by the youngest, a director. Then one year the youngest couldn't come on the annual trip. The older peacekeeper said, 'We spent the entire weekend trying to decide what to do!'

The Quiet Witness

The peacekeeper's witnessing style naturally will be quite different from a director's or an entertainer's. You might find peacekeepers amid a large group who are telling

Christ's message by going door to door, passing out tracts at the airport, or giving testimonies at a retreat full of strangers, but rarely will they do any of these willingly or happily. Peacekeepers may struggle to get conversations going with total strangers, but they can have a profound impact on family and neighbours through personal or friendship evangelism. My friend Leanne's steady faith, gentle nature and daily commitment to Christ and to her family kept me going to church and inspired me to seek God during a period of years when I would otherwise have given up on my faith.

If you reflect on your life and why you are a Christian, you are quite likely to discover that several peacekeepers helped lead the way. Doris Clements, affectionately called 'Clem' by thirty teenagers at my home church during the mid-seventies, is the name that stands out most in my mind. Clem was the youth-group leader and organist who had unfailing love, patience, generosity and kindness. She would talk with you, give you a ride to or from church or just spend time with you. She never said no to anyone. In the days before seat-belt laws, her blue saloon was often packed with kids en route to a youth rally, a weekend retreat or the local take-away.

Where would the world be without the soothing, calming, loving influence of peacekeepers?

5

The Analyser

The analyser is a cautious conservative with an eye for detail. This meticulous personality can assess pages of data, calculate columns of figures and patiently and happily look for typographical errors in the London telephone directory. Perfectionists to the nth degree, analysers actually read the directions that come with new electronic gadgets *before* they plug them in and turn them on.

While the flashy entertainer wears the latest fashions and the hottest new colours, the low-key analyser is happiest wearing the same conservative colours in classic styles. During the early years of our marriage, my analyser husband dressed so conservatively he looked as if he'd been born middle-aged. Several years of insisting and encouraging (and nagging) got him finally to break away from his plain white shirts. He's come a long way – now he occasionally wears yellow, cream and light blue! But Mike still draws the line if I bring home anything that remotely resembles purple.

Analysers cling to their conservative dress to mask their number one fear: embarrassment. Entertainers are happy for people to talk about them, no matter what they say; directors don't notice or care what anyone says; and peacekeepers avoid drawing any comments in the first place. But the analyser considers any criticism to be an almost mortal wound. To avoid making mistakes that could cause censure, and therefore embarrassment, the analyser will go through extensive preparation to maintain accuracy.

Details, Details, Details!

Analysers are needed on every project, committee and task force. They don't like surprises, so they ask questions the rest of us don't even think about, such as the following: Could hidden costs arise? Where? What subcommittees do we set up? How many people will attend the event? How will we publicise? How much, if anything, should we charge? What would make the event worth while from the attendees' point of view? What topics should we cover? Will we need refreshments? When would we plug in the coffee-pot? Should we offer baby-sitting services? What could go wrong with our plan? The list goes on.

One analyser or another always seems to clean up my messes. When I offered to bring a pile of pumpkins to the church retreat on Hallowe'en weekend, analysers came to the rescue, supplying necessities I hadn't considered, such as newspapers to spread under the pumpkins, markers to draw the faces, knives to carve and candles to put in the finished jack-o'-lanterns.

Analysers notice details *everywhere*. Our portrait studio has a heavily used hallway between the front door and the camera room. Mike put a carpet runner down to prevent the wall-to-wall carpet from getting worn. Naturally, after a few years the runner started looking scruffy. Mike wanted to replace it since no amount of scrubbing would get it clean. I objected to the purchase because it seemed like a pretty boring thing to spend money on, plus it was just going to get dirty again anyway. Mike pointed out that not everyone was a director like me and that the stained runner would bother at least 25 per cent of the clients who walked through the front door. We bought the runner.

This attention to detail extends to our vehicles. I would be happy to hose down my car once or twice a year. After all, it will just get dirty again! Fortunately, analyser Mike routinely sets the alarm clock several times a week to get the car and truck spotless before he has to go to the office. When the hose is out of action because the ground is frozen, Mike may even haul buckets of water to and from the kitchen sink. When his father was visiting us one Christmas, the two analysers took our vehicle to a full-service indoor car wash. It seemed futile to me, since the ground was covered with snow and ice and the accompanying sand and salt. But if only for a few moments, the jeep was clean, and the men were happy.

With an inborn penchant for perfection, the analyser has the potential to be among the most gifted artists or musicians. Consider Michelangelo and his statue of David. A director would have made a few last whacks, called the statue good enough, checked it off his list and moved on to the next project. The entertainer would have been side-tracked chatting with the model, other artists working nearby or the cleaner who came to sweep up the chippings. The statue would never have been completed. The easygoing peacekeeper, overwhelmed at the enormity of the task, would not have been able to decide when, where or how to begin. The statue would never have been started. Only a perfectionist analyser would have gone to the mortuary and cut up bodies just to study the way muscles look. Not only did analyser Michelangelo thoroughly prepare *before* he began, but he had the patience and the perseverance to work until he had perfected the statue.

I saw this analyser trait up close when I was giving a

lecture away from home. My fellow speaker, who hailed from the area, took me to visit a childhood friend who was a sculptor. He was busy working on the hand of a life-sized statue of a wealthy patron's daughter. The sculptor planned to stay up all night to get the hand just right because the patron was due to check up on the work's progress first thing in the morning. The hand looked flawless to me; I couldn't see what improvements he could possibly make that would be worth losing a night's sleep over!

Perfectionism, of course, is found beyond the arts. Curt, a professional customer-service speaker, responded to his pastor's call for volunteers to share testimonies at an approaching Lenten service. Curt wrote on the back of a Communion card and dropped it in the offering to let the pastor know. Then he went directly from church to his office to draft the message. After three hours at the computer, he filed the written testimony so he could refer back to it when the pastor called. When I made a similar offer at our church, I waited until a few days before to jot a few words down on a single index card. Curt offered his message from the podium just about verbatim, while I delivered mine ad lib from the centre aisle. I probably looked as though I was speaking off the top of my head, but Curt's delivery must have looked well polished.

This passion for perfection spills over into every facet of daily living, from cereals to stereos. There is only one cereal my husband, Mike, finds worth eating, since it alone has 100 per cent of his daily vitamin requirements. 'If you're going to eat cereal,' he says, 'it might as well be the best.' Our entertainer son, Jason, whose motto is 'If It Feels Good, Do It', only wants to eat cereal that tastes good. While Mike's being nutritious and Jason's eating junk, I'm exercising my taste for continual change by systematically eating my way through a variety pack. And I don't think my peacekeeper friend ever had time to eat cereal of any kind during our growing-up years. She stayed in bed till the very last minute and was lucky if she made it to school on time.

These sorts of differences show up in our choice of stereo components. In true analyser style, Mike only wants the best of the best. His idea of a good time is to climb to the attic to rewire his stereo speakers for 'optimum listening enjoyment'. Entertainer Jason doesn't care about the quality of the system as long as he can crank up the volume when his friends are over. Try as I might, I just don't notice the sound difference. My peacekeeper friend is happy with her basic cassette recorder and sees no need to buy a quality stereo.

Doers and Doubters

God calls us to do his work based on our special strengths, and Noah is a great example of an analyser. God called Noah to build an ark, not to be a leader like director Paul or a smooth-talking spokesperson like entertainers Aaron and Peter. With lists of specific details on building the ark, plus the tedious work of gathering the animals and food for the voyage, God needed a personality he could depend on.

Had God called a director, the ark would have been quickly slapped together without *all* the directions necessarily being followed. An entertainer at the helm would have had trouble ignoring all the taunts and jeers from the crowd of onlookers and other distractions also would have interfered with the production deadline. A peacekeeper would have been overwhelmed at the enormity of the task. He wouldn't have known how to tackle it and might have had difficulty delegating tasks to others. The boat would never have made it out of dry dock. Noah not only made the deadline, he followed God's instructions to the letter.

God used Gideon not to build but to destroy. Gideon tore down the altars of Baal and eased Israel's suffering under the Midianites. Gideon may have been destined to be a great warrior, prophet and judge, but he had to get over a serious case of the jitters first. Typical of an analyser, he wanted proof. When the angel of the Lord first spoke to Gideon, he responded by requesting a sign. God awed Gideon by bringing fire down from heaven to consume Gideon's offering of food and drink. Although Gideon acknowledged him as God, he still tested the Lord twice more, putting a fleece outside overnight and asking God to make it wet while leaving the ground around it dry, then asking that the fleece be left dry while the ground around got wet. Talk about testing the Lord! But the Lord patiently granted Gideon the surety he asked for.

Analyser Hannah showed her faith and devotion by dedicating her son, Samuel, to the Lord's service. Although he was her only child, she offered him to God in appreciation for answering her prayers. He was enlisted in temple service when he was just three. Hannah faithfully made him a coat each year, which she brought to him on her annual visits.

Timothy was quite likely an analyser. As a young man he was filled with the self-doubt typical of the cautious, conservative analyser. Paul called him wise and took him under his wing. Timothy ultimately became a great defender of the faith. His attention to detail made his ministry dynamic and his writings above question. Paul commended him on his ability to serve flawlessly (Phil. 2:20–23).

My analyser husband, Mike, is much like Timothy. Timothy learned the Scriptures in his early years from his mother Eunice and his grandmother Lois; Mike spent twelve years attending church school. To both Mike and Timothy, faithfully raised in the church, belief in God was a given. They didn't doubt God. They doubted themselves. Timothy was worried that he was too young and inexperienced. He was certain no one would listen to him. The great leap of faith for the analyser Christian is to believe in the gifts and blessings of God enough to use them for God's glory.

A Case of the 'Yes, Buts'

As with all the personality types, the weaknesses of the analyser are an offshoot of the strengths. The tendency to doubt tops the list. The hard-core analyser believes anything and everything is too good to be true. Analysers know if they poke around just below the surface, they will find the problems that are sure to exist. In a word, they are *pessimistic*. Doom and gloom surround this pernickety personality, who is always expecting something to go wrong.

The director maintains a pretty upbeat attitude; the entertainer quickly alternates between mood extremes; and the peacekeeper maintains a moderate status quo. But analysers are prone to deep depressions. Once the mood descends, no amount of cajoling, humouring or badgering will lift their spirits.

Perfection is another analyser plus with a tendency to swing to a drawback. Since these cautious conservatives set such high standards, they put off taking any action until everything is just right. Also, since they set such lofty (often unrealistic) goals, they are often disappointed when they don't reach them. Where other personalities would regroup and set new goals, analysers consider themselves inadequate failures. This all-or-nothing philosophy makes analysers put aside their special gifts and talents unless they can be the best in their field. Obviously, since they cannot all start at the top, many analysers never exercise their gifts at all.

Analysers run into problems with one-to-one people skills when they care more about the details of completing the project correctly than about their co-workers. They also harbour grudges for years, often for an offence that was nothing in the eyes of the offender.

The analyser handles pressure in a particular way. Where the director gets bossy, the entertainer gets sarcastic and the peacekeeper gives in, analysers will withdraw from civilisation. In short, they take their gloomy black cloud down the landing to the bedroom, close the door and wallow in self-pity.

You can spot analyser children by their periodic dark clouds and the low profile they maintain. I used to point out a particular boy we would regularly see walking to school while we were driving to work. He walked with his hands in his pockets and his shoulders drooping. He always looked at the ground, never glancing up to see who or what was around him. It was almost as if he was trying to blend into the pavement so he could get to school as unnoticed as possible. Finally I told my analyser husband that the boy looked as I imagined Mike must have looked when he was walking to school as a child. Looking at him, Mike replied, 'Exactly.'

Another analyser trait you can easily spot in children is how intently they get involved with interests. When an analyser gets into something, he really gets into it. As a child, Mike left a trail of hobbies. You could always tell what he was interested in, because he was absorbed in it to the exclusion of all else. The family still tells stories about the fish tanks he scattered throughout the house, including the six-by-four-foot aquarium he had in his bedroom, complete with a cascading waterfall. Next came model gliders. Then short-wave radios. Then the darkroom he built in a shed behind the house. Boxes filled with all the clutter from his childhood hobbies are gradually making their way across country from his parents' attic to our cellar.

Another noticeable trait of analysers is that they never throw anything away. The only way I can clean cupboards is to wait until Mike goes away for a few days. I have to resort to similar tactics at the studio. But Mike has still retrieved all kinds of things that I've tried to throw out: damaged frames he might use for kindling, sample portraits that are scratched and faded, on which he might mount a new print, and out-of-date catalogues that he might use for price comparison. My director motto is 'When in Doubt, Throw It Out.' Mike's analyser motto is 'You Never Know When You Might Need It.'

The 'Doubting Thomas' Profile

Who hasn't heard the story of Thomas? This poor apostle has had a bad press for nearly two thousand years because, like all analysers, he wanted hard evidence. He's not the only biblical sceptic. Zechariah took some convincing when an angel told him that his aged and barren wife, Elizabeth, would conceive a child (Luke 1:18). The Queen of Sheba made a twelve-hundred-mile camel journey to see the wisdom of King Solomon. She could have sent an ambassador, but this courageous analyser wanted to see for herself (2 Chr. 9). Your church and community are, no doubt, filled with analysers like Thomas who look for evidence that God is alive and truly what he claims to be.

Betty, an analyser who was brought up in the Methodist Church, said she went 'very intellectual' during her secondary-school years. The minister tried to get her involved in the youth group, but she told him she wasn't interested. At college many of her peers happened to be Christian, and she literally went to every church in that small university town, attending each week with a different friend. With support like this Betty's scepticism slowly diminished. 'These Christian friends would show up at the oddest times just to offer a bit of encouragement and to show that they cared,' she remarked. 'I came to know Christ through the collective witness of all these friends.'

In Curt's testimony at the Lenten service, he explained that he had struggled to believe and accept God. As he closed his testimony, he said, 'It's frightening to think how easy it would have been to just say no. I would have missed out on the opportunity God was offering me. I was supposed to receive God's Word. And right now I am supposed to be here, sharing my faith with others. It's quite a thought!'

Study Questions, Chapters 1–5

1. Which of the people in the following list responded the way you would in a similar situation? How?
2. What strengths do you have in common?
3. What weaknesses?
4. Make a list of your other strengths and weaknesses.

Directors

1. Paul: Acts 9:1–31; 18:9–11; 23:11; 26:1–32.
2. Jezebel: 1 Kings 18:18–19; 19:1–2; 21:7–11; 2 Kings 9:30–37.

Entertainers

1. Peter: Matthew 14:25–31; John 18:10–11, 15–17, 25–27; Acts 2:2–4, 13–42.
2. Aaron: Exodus 4:14–16; 32:1–6.

Peacekeepers
1. Ruth: Ruth 1:16–17; 3:5–11.
2. Eli: 1 Samuel 3:10–14; 4:14–22.
Analysers
1. Noah: Genesis 6:6–22; 7:1–24.
2. Thomas: John 11:11–16; 14:1–7; 20:24–29.

6

How Others Hear Your Message

We're actually getting off pretty lightly with the Great Commission. All Jesus asks of us is to tell the world about the true meaning of Easter. The Holy Spirit has the greater task of providing the burden of truth and softening the hardened human heart to let in the love of Christ. Our part is to behave and speak in ways that will help, not hinder, the Spirit.

We cannot expect people to go from wondering if God even exists one minute to accepting Christ as Lord and Saviour the next. They need to do a lot of thinking between the two stages. While the Spirit works, we too can continually work to create a desire in them to hear the message. We are called to help people *want* to seek God and claim his promise: 'You will seek me and find me when you seek me with all your heart' (Jer. 29:13).

To give someone the desire to seek God, we need to be able to communicate what it is we want them to think about. We need to present our message in terms that particular personality can relate to.

'Be wise in the way you act towards outsiders; make the most of every opportunity. Let your conversation be always full of grace, seasoned with salt, so that you may know how to answer everyone' (Col. 4:5). How can we begin to have the right answer for everyone if we don't know what or why we believe? How can we be wise in all our contacts with them if we cannot communicate effectively by understanding the personality variables of those we're witnessing to?

Sharing my vision of Christ is similar to sharing my portrait photography 'eye' with my clients. Before I actually arrange a photo session, I sit down with them and show them a wide range of samples. I want to find out what they like and what they don't like. Based on their comments, we choose a location and style that suits their tastes.

If I launched right into the photography without first finding out about their preferences, I couldn't properly meet their needs; I would shoot my favourite styles at the location I chose with the type of film I like. They might want a formal portrait taken with colour film against a traditional painted backdrop, but I would deliver a casual portrait taken with black-and-white film at the beach.

By taking the time to get to know the clients personally, I successfully match my menu of choices to their individual needs. One key reason I can create the desire for my product is that I know all the little variables for all the portrait styles I offer. If you were to ask me any question about any of the possibilities, I could give you a detailed answer.

It seems common sense for anyone in business to have this type of product knowledge. And even though personal evangelism is not a business, common sense is valuable in that area as well. After all, you're exercising good communication skills when you match what you know about the love of Jesus Christ with the needs and interests of the person to whom you're witnessing.

Some might call this concept 'manipulation', but that is not the case at all. If you can't get past the outer personality, how can you expect the person to *listen to*, let alone *hear*, the message about the love of Jesus Christ?

Models of Perfection

Ideal personalities – composites of all the strengths of the four personality profiles – show us a goal to aim for ourselves and in our relations with other profiles. The Bible offers two examples of the perfect person.

In Proverbs 31:10–31 the author extols the values of the virtuous woman. Twenty-two verses offer an admirable portrait of the perfect wife and mother. While every woman will see a little of herself in this model, it may be hard for us to relate to because it *is* ideal and seemingly impossible to duplicate. This, however, does not lessen the model's worth. Look at it as a challenge to stretch your strengths.

Jesus is the New Testament example of the perfect person. During his time on earth, he was a tangible example of the best traits of the four personality profiles. He was a born leader who boldly spoke with authority and conviction and who thrived on challenge and change. He was popular with people because he was friendly and spontaneous – not above turning water into wine at a wedding celebration. He entertained (and taught) people for entire days with his storytelling finesse. Though the extrovert side of Jesus attracted people, they remained drawn to him because they respected his compassion, loyalty, serenity and wisdom in resolving disputes. Even the scribes and Pharisees envied his command of language and of the Scriptures and his clear, purposeful approach to teaching about God.

Christ's life and his death testify that his witness matched his words; and his resurrection powerfully persuades us that striving to be like him is a worthy goal.

New Christians have great expectations of assuming Christ's personality within seconds of accepting him as Lord and Saviour. The world expects much the same. For example, when I was a guest at a New Year's Eve party a few years ago I grew upset with how the hosts' children were treating our son. Rather than bite my tongue and keep the matter to myself for a more appropriate time, I lashed out in my most hateful director mode. The hosts and I had several telephone conversations in the following weeks as I tried to mend our friendship. One comment really stung: 'And you call yourself a *Christian*!' In addition to my own mortification for acting like an idiot, I felt the remorse of falsely representing Jesus Christ.

So what is the answer? How do we balance our desire to serve and follow Christ on one hand while we bungle things on the other? First, we can allow the Holy Spirit to work in our life to temper our temperament. Second, we can learn as much as we can about the human elements of our own personality. Third, we can discover how to balance our personality with the personalities of the rest of the world.

We know that we *should* be like Christ, and we also know that we often fail. Add to that the fact that life would be pretty dull if we all spoke and responded the same. Obviously we can't and shouldn't expect perfection in all our witnessing experiences. So when someone dares to offer a different opinion or misunderstands how you explain your views, expect it – you'll save yourself a lot of frustration.

When you try to find the best way to share your message, don't expect one approach to work with everybody. Each personality sends and receives differently, and you must tailor your talk to the other person. The first step is to accept the fact that people are different. By now you probably agree with this basic concept.

The next step is to realise that your personality is not *the* perfect personality. That is another pretty basic concept – but one we cannot brush aside. Unfortunately we too often do because we're afraid of our flaws.

We had a pretty lively group discussion on this topic during a two-family camping trip last April. Four adults were seated around the picnic table by the campfire. We represented each of the four personality styles. Lynn, the entertainer, didn't like her list of weaknesses at all. She was certain it was much worse than any other. The annoying habits topping her list were that she talks too much, has a restless energy and has trouble finishing tasks. Meanwhile, her husband, Peter, was not keen on his list of peacekeeper negatives, which included things like 'indecisive', 'unenthusiastic' and 'stubborn about changes'. Mike said his analyser list wasn't much better; it included 'moody', 'depressed' and 'hard to please'. I quickly pointed out the familiar word on my list: 'bossy'. It also included 'impatient', 'inflexible' and 'quick-tempered'.

When we compared notes, we all realised that the other lists didn't look as bad because a difficult issue for an entertainer (like talking too much) would be a piece of cake for a peacekeeper, who has the opposite problem.

Even an outside observer could quickly identify the personality differences of this foursome by watching casual conversation, because the key communication element for each personality is different. The director wants to tell you what to do, the entertainer wants to tell you about him or herself, the peacekeeper doesn't want to talk at all, and the analyser wants to sit back and study the overall conversation before deciding whether the topic is worthy of any input.

It takes a conscious effort to break this pattern. When someone says to me that people can change personality styles over the years, I suggest sitting back and studying the conversation patterns of friends and family. No matter how much anyone tries to change, the core personality resurfaces: the director will always try to control the conversation, the entertainer will always talk the most, the peacekeeper will avoid talking altogether and the analyser will take a long time before offering an opinion.

If the conversation gets too heated, the personality factor takes on a slightly different twist. The director will be at his or her bossiest, often lashing out without thinking things through. The entertainer will attack the opposition with comments coated in sarcasm. The peacekeeper will either avoid the confrontation by letting the big mouths take over or dredge up old wrongs and use them as ammunition for the present. The analyser will avoid the pressure problem by retreating (sometimes physically) into a thick cloud of doom and gloom.

The only way to break the ugly cycle of overreacting is to take a deep breath, *reflect* on what you should say and do (not on how you want to react), and then *respond* accordingly. Only then will you sense that your personality is 'changing'.

When to Break the Golden Rule

The childhood game of Chinese Whispers is the ideal example of how differently we listen, hear and respond. To play, everyone sits on the floor in a circle. The leader whispers a sentence to the person seated to the right, and the message gradually travels around the circle. The last person says the sentence out loud to whoops of laughter – because the final sentence rarely resembles what the leader originally whispered.

If this happens in a simple game when we are trying hard

to hear the correct message, it will happen even more noticeably in day-to-day conversations when our minds are drifting from focus to focus and we aren't concentrating on what the speaker is saying. In our witnessing, communication is the biggest challenge. Since we don't want the message to change, we must perfect how we send it.

The Golden Rule says, 'Do unto others as you would have them do unto you.' This is good as far as it goes. But more accurately, people want to be treated how *they* (not you) want to be treated! (How you would like to be treated may be very different from how they would like to be treated.) Therefore, the 'Golden Rule' of witnessing is 'Do unto others as they would have you do unto them.' Each personality style will want something different. As Florence Littauer explains in *Personality Plus*, while the entertainer is talking, the director is doing and achieving, the peacekeeper is watching, and the analyser is thinking, planning, creating and inventing. Each personality processes new information – in our case the gospel – in and around all of these activities.

'You have to practise basic relationship skills in general to be a better witness,' explains Robert L. Burgess, a speaker and consultant who specialises in communication skills and the Personal Profile System. 'The idea is reflection. You *reflect back* what you see. You may need to slow down a few notches, lower your tone of speech, and ask the other person questions. You can't motivate anyone to do something for your reasons. You must look at life, and the message of Jesus Christ, through their eyes.'

Burgess points out that even God reaches people where and how they need to be reached based on their personality.

> [Director] Saul needed to be confronted, so God knocked him off a horse on the way to Damascus. [Analyser] Moses

needed God to *prove* he was in fact God. [Entertainer] Peter needed to develop a strong relationship with Jesus and then learn that the relationship was more important than personal popularity. God chose what [peacekeeper] Abraham valued most, his family, to test and challenge him.

Successfully mixing and matching our own personality style with others takes a combination of common sense and practice. As an outspoken director, I tend to talk fast and to the point, assuming the other person is moderately familiar with whatever topic I may be explaining. When I'm relating with another director, I can do this. However, I must slow my pace and modify my approach when witnessing to peacekeepers, or I will intimidate them. Many times I've forgotten this and gabbed merrily along in a lopsided conversation until a peacekeeper says, 'Read my lips, Helen. You are talking too fast! Slow down!' If I don't slow my pace, I may as well never bother to share my message because it won't be heard.

Likewise, the slow, steady nature of the peacekeeper can be infuriating for the fast-paced director. Unless the peacekeeper steps up the pace, the director won't wait to listen. The director's mind will be racing ahead to what to cook for supper, when the annual report copy is due, and how to juggle the already too-crowded timetable to squeeze in a five-mile jog.

A similar communication problem occurs when a meticulous analyser provides too much detail when witnessing to an easygoing entertainer. When the situation is turned about, the chatterbox entertainer needs to stop the lengthy dissertation about his or her own salvation experience and offer the analyser detailed facts and proofs about Jesus Christ and his resurrection.

The examples below, and in the next four chapters, offer a starting point for more effectively communicating the gospel with other personalities. The suggestions are meant to be broad-based and simple to illustrate the more striking differences between personalities. The concept is similar to professional photographers creating images that follow the basic rules of composition, design, colour harmony and so forth. When you know the rules and your subject well, you may choose to break a rule to come up with a better picture.

Once you understand the heart and soul of what a certain personality needs to hear, you can break the rules. An entertainer may desire a deeper emotional experience than you expected, or a peacekeeper may ask to hear the factual elements of Christ's death and resurrection. Flexibility and adaptability are good once you have a feel for relating to different personalities.

Tip Sheet for Witnessing to the Four Personalities

When you're sharing with a director . . .

- keep the message short
- get to the point quickly
- define what being a Christian is all about
- emphasise that Christianity is a 'smart choice'

When you're sharing with an entertainer . . .

- make it obvious you're interested in him or her
- emphasise the positive
- keep the details to a minimum
- help overcome fear of 'what others will say'

When you're sharing with a peacekeeper . . .

- establish personal rapport first
- show genuine concern
- emphasise the personal relationship aspect of knowing Christ
- show patience by giving the person time

When you're sharing with an analyser . . .

- know exactly what you are talking about
- keep your facts straight
- emphasise historical data (via apologetics)
- ask and answer lots of questions so the person can draw his or her own conclusions

The best way to begin witnessing is with the aspect of Jesus Christ that's most relevant to the person and the situation – his character, personality, earthly life or purpose in the resurrection. One of the keynote speakers at Congress 1991, a gathering of five thousand Christians, talked about the person who had repeatedly shared the message of Jesus Christ with him while he was a student. The outspoken entertainer said, 'I didn't want to hear about his Jesus, but I did want him to help me with my Latin homework. That was where my pain was, and that was where he met me!'

The task before us is to use personality-profile information to meet the unsaved person's pain with the love of Jesus Christ.

7

Witnessing to the Director

'Because of his kindness you have been saved through trusting Christ. And even trusting is not of yourselves; it too is a gift from God. Salvation is not a reward for the good we have done, so none of us can take any credit for it' (Eph. 2:8–9 LB).

While most personalities will look at these verses and assume the word 'good' refers to such things as charity, kindness, hospitality and grace, the director *knows* Paul is writing about more tangible accomplishments. Directors will be equally confident that heaven's gates will be thrown open for them and that a great welcome banner will wave in honour of the lengthy list of wonderful feats they have completed.

This confidence is one of the greatest obstacles you will have to overcome when you witness to a director, because the inborn belief 'I can make it on my own' is the primary chasm separating this motivated leader from accepting Christ as Lord and Saviour. At any sales-training seminar you will be told, 'There are two kinds of thinkers in life – those who think they can and those who think they can't. They are both right.' Of course, directors go beyond just *thinking* they are right. They *know* it and quickly set out to *prove* it!

Dealing with the Issues

Directors plan to prove they can go it alone. Since they are set on this goal, the last thing they want to do is give up their authority and prestige and submit to the will of God. So it isn't that directors *can't* believe; they *won't* believe. Some might call this the original sin inherent in all people, but the problem is intensified with directors because of their strong self-will. They *choose* not to believe, and they turn their backs on God.

Many claim to have 'intellectual problems' with the Christian faith, but their problems are not of the mind but the will. (For the director who is even mildly interested in the intellectual side, plenty of information is available to reveal the credibility and reliability of Jesus Christ.) They know that once they acknowledge the reality of Christ, they are responsible for examining the sin in their lives. Since most directors are happily working their way to the top ten of the Success Unlimited chart, they've got better things to do. It is much easier to stick with the 'intellectual problem' about believing in Christ. It sounds good, and it feels safe!

Other directors claim that God does not exist. Often people do not believe in God because they don't have the slightest idea who God is or what Christianity is all about. You can help fill in the blanks there. Fortunately, no one believes in nothing. Everyone has faith in someone or something. The atheist's dilemma also plays into your hands: people feel grateful, want to express appreciation, but have no one to thank. C. S. Lewis talks about atheism in *Mere Christianity*. 'Atheism turns out to be too simple,' he says. 'If the whole universe has no meaning, we should have never found out that it has no meaning; just as, if there were no light in the universe and therefore no creatures with eyes, we should never know it is dark. "Dark" would be without meaning.'

Two other stones directors love to hurl are aimed at believers: 'If Christianity is so great, why are there so few Christians?' and 'I've seen too many hypocrites.'

Jesus answers the first in Matthew 7:13–14: 'Enter through the narrow gate. For wide is the gate and broad is the road that leads to destruction, and many enter through it. But small is the gate and narrow the road that leads to life, and only a few find it.' The easiest route through life leads to hell.

Zig Ziglar likes to throw the hypocrite comment right back by saying, 'Come on down to church. We always have room for one more!'

Of course, the real issue to relay to the 'I can make it on my own' director is what God says about making it to heaven on your own. We like to compare ourselves to each other so we come out looking good, but God compares us to Jesus Christ. Next to him, we don't even come close. Christianity doesn't rise or fall on the way a Christian acts today or yesterday, but on the person of Jesus Christ. He was not a hypocrite.

Setting Up Your Strategy

It can be pretty intimidating to witness to a director, because this personality *coined* the word 'intimidation'! Keep in mind that a successful director is not necessarily better than everyone else. Directors' success usually can be traced back to their willingness to work longer and harder at reaching their goals. They don't have more skills. They simply have more drive.

Pastor Tim LaHaye, in his bestselling classic *Spirit-*

Controlled Temperament, says it's critical to witness to a director during the early school years. The director will fight the Holy Spirit the hardest and longest. As the years go by, with each secular success this self-sufficient soul will feel less and less of a need to seek the kingdom of God.

If you can't witness to your director friends, neighbours or relatives before they reach their teens, you need to be prepared to witness on their turf and on their terms.

You don't need to be bosom pals to share your faith with directors. They are most comfortable in a businesslike, efficient, professional atmosphere. Anything sentimental will send them running. Make sure you have your material prepared in advance. Groping for answers will make you appear incompetent, irritating this fast-paced and impatient personality. Stick to the facts. Directors want to know what Christianity is, what makes it different from other religions and why they should waste their time with it. Since directors like dealing with specific tasks more than relationships, the intangible aspects of Christianity will be more difficult to explain. You will also have to help the director with learning how to give control over to God.

Robert L. Burgess, the author and consultant who specialises in personality and communication skills, offers these suggestions:

> Step up the pace a few notches and emphasize the rightness, correctness, and impact of making a decision to accept Jesus Christ. You might say, 'I know it's important when you make a decision, you need to make a strong one that you can really rely on.'
>
> Since the chain of command is understood and considered very important, you can share the story of the Roman centurion who came to Jesus. That is a [director]

approach since they respect authority. You might say something like, 'When you've been under the authority of someone else, they made a decision that you didn't understand. It might even have been your parents. When you looked back later, you realized it was the right decision. Think of yourself in that scenario with God as the person in charge who is making that right decision. All faith is is putting your hand in the hand of someone else who has the full picture. It is much better to give your faith to someone who has the full picture than to someone who cannot and does not see the full picture.

As the inevitable disagreements arise, don't argue feelings. To maintain the director's respect and attention, it is imperative that you stick to the facts. You might remind the director that decision-making is based on *probability* and not certainty. Even Pascal said the first function of reason is to show people that some things are beyond reason! We make most decisions based on a combination of faith and the facts we do know. We cry out for absolute certainty in religious matters, but we don't (and can't) expect it. Faith must come into play.

Even while Jesus was with his disciples and followers, they struggled to find the faith he expected of them. In Mark 9 we read that while Jesus was away the disciples failed to cast out demons from a boy. When Jesus came, the boy's father asked him to heal his son if he could. '"If you can?" said Jesus. "Everything is possible for him who believes." Immediately the boy's father exclaimed, "I do believe; help me overcome my unbelief!"' (Mark 9:23–24).

Marcelle, an octogenarian from my church, describes faith this way, 'If someone says, "Prove it!" that is not faith. Faith is something you do not see, but something you feel.' Her definition of faith is similar to what is written in the first verse of Hebrews 11: 'Now faith is being sure of what we hope for and certain of what we do not see.' While this might not be enough of an answer for some Christians, it is the answer for director Marcelle.

She relates her own pig-headed struggle to find and accept faith. Born in Paris during World War I, Marcelle was educated at a Christian boarding school outside the war-torn city. The school had a Communion service every morning and prayers every evening. Although the foundation for faith was laid day after day during her school years, her faith did not become real until 1950, when she had cancer.

'I had been doing all the church work – missions, visiting the housebound, doing services at the nursing homes – but I never had really faced God,' Marcelle admits. 'The minister called and said, "I'm going to pray for one thing and one thing only – that you will accept whatever God has for you." I was so furious with him! For the next few days, all that was going through my mind was how to accept what God had in store for me.

'I finally did turn my will over to God and accept what he had for me,' Marcelle says. 'From there my faith grew. *Proof* is a mathematical problem solved. *Faith* is what you feel within your heart.'

Oswald Chambers offers a similar viewpoint in *My Utmost for His Highest*: 'Faith is not intelligent understanding, faith is deliberate commitment to a person where I see no way.'

A byproduct of faith that appeals to every director is what Norman Vincent Peale called a 'non-emotionalized reaction to any problem'. He said when the fear element is reduced, through faith, you can think more clearly and more objectively. You can see the facts as they are, and you don't have to worry about your emotions colouring or clouding your vision. Marcelle simply calls this 'faith with power'!

Love, Don't Preach

'Love, don't preach' might seem contradictory to the thick-skinned nature of the director, but a particularly strong witness will be from a loving, caring, honest director to the less loving, less caring, less honest non-Christian counterpart. Everyone is inundated with the rules of life. The void we all sense within our hearts is love. God created us because he wanted a race to love him. In order for this love to be real, we were given the option to choose. Because we have the choice between good and bad, the possibility and reality of evil are on the edge of our every decision.

When anyone chooses love over evil, people notice. When a director chooses right over wrong, it is a particularly profound statement to the rest of the world's dominant personalities. If an unsaved director will not listen to your verbal testimony, he or she cannot ignore your tempered tongue, gentled nature and impeccable business practices.

That Stubborn Will

Despite all the evidence readily available about Jesus the Son of God, all that many directors will agree on is that he was a great moral teacher. To this C. S. Lewis responds in *Mere Christianity*:

> A man who was merely a man and said the sort of things Jesus said would not be a great moral teacher. He would either be a lunatic – on a level with the man who says he is a poached egg – or else he would be the Devil of Hell.

> You must make your choice. Either this man was, and is, the Son of God; or else a madman or something else.
>
> You can shut Him up for a fool, you can spit at Him and kill Him as a demon; or you can fall at His feet and call Him Lord and God. But let us not come up with any patronizing nonsense about His being a great human teacher. He has not left that open to us. He did not intend to.

You must help the director decide whether Jesus's claim to be God was true or false. To paraphrase Lewis, if the director agrees that it is a true claim, the next choice is whether to accept or reject that truth. If the director decides the claim is false, he is calling Jesus a liar or a madman. By denying Christ's claim, the director is pointing his finger at Jesus as one who deliberately set out to lie and deceive his followers. If not that, then Jesus was totally out of his mind. His 'delusion' about being God cost him his life when a simple denial would have kept him from the cross.

With all of this information logically presented to directors, they will consistently come up against the issue of their stubborn will. Madeline sat on the front row of a workshop I gave one year at 'Women in the Word'. She spoke of her struggle with jealousy and her iron will. From age four to about thirteen, she regularly attended church and Sunday school. About that time a friend who was a year younger went for a week at a Word of Life summer camp. She came back with an exuberance for life, and Madeline immediately noticed a big change in her. 'My friend was a little more mischievous than I was. She was also a year younger than I. I felt jealousy and rejection that God would use her first,' Madeline told me. 'I gradually stopped going to church to the point that I was agnostic for fourteen years.'

Then one Monday evening Madeline cried out to the Lord, telling him of her unhappiness and confusion. She didn't really know what she was looking for. The following Friday evening the same friend from so many years ago phoned and wanted to call in to see her.

'I had been taking Catholic instruction, but I made a mental note *not* to mention it because I didn't want to give her an opening to talk about Christianity,' explained the stubborn director.

'There was a lot of light coming from her. After we had said our goodbyes, I heard myself saying I was taking Catholic instruction. She said she had had a strong nudge all week long to phone me. She said she promised God she would go to see me, but she would only talk about religion if I brought it up first!'

Madeline remembered that during the months and years when she was wilfully running from God, she felt rootless. 'It was like being on a round-the-world trip and wanting to get off at home, but the plane just wouldn't land. I know there were several times that I went round and had the chance to get off, but I didn't because I was being so stubborn.'

Not by Might but by Spirit

'"Not by [Director] might, nor by [Director] power, but by my Spirit," says the LORD Almighty' (Zech. 4:6).

'I am the vine; you are the branches. If a man remains in me and I in him, he will bear much fruit; apart from me you can do nothing' (John 15:5).

A director may read these verses a thousand times, but the message to give up the controls and let God take over does not easily get under the thick skin of confidence.

Meredith, an aggressive professional who calls herself a director/entertainer, explains her struggle with these verses.

'I am from a very dysfunctional family, but I played "perfect" all my life. I was the perfect daughter, the perfect teenager and the perfect student and churchgoer. What people didn't know was that I was living a lie.

'I was a secret alcoholic; I began drinking when I was only thirteen. My father was an alcoholic, and I am a survivor of incest. I was also raped when I was nineteen. In college I was very promiscuous, and I was always partying and drinking. When I was at university, I got pregnant and I didn't even know who the father was. I got out the razor blades and the beer, and I was going to end it all.'

Meredith didn't slice into her wrists right away because she kept getting flashbacks to all her years of attending Sunday school and confirmation class. 'I thought it was all a lie when I was sitting in those classes, but somehow the words must have got through. The words of different Sunday-school teachers were filling my head, literally coming out of nowhere. I remembered verses and phrases perfectly. They were as clear as if they were being spoken right there in the room with me.

'I got down on my knees and prayed for Jesus Christ to come into my heart. I felt like I had been reborn. I felt like a different person, like I had hope.' Meredith finally found the message of Philippians 4:6–7: 'Do not be anxious about anything, but in everything, by prayer and petition, with thanksgiving, present your requests to God. And the peace of God, which transcends all understanding, will guard your hearts and your minds in Christ Jesus.'

The story of the prodigal son (Luke 15:11–32) is an ideal illustration for directors who, like Meredith and Madeline, just won't give in. Not only did the son come to his senses intellectually (by comparing his pig slops to his father's table), he also took action and made the journey home.

Witnessing to the Director Round-Up Questions

1. Visualise director friends, relatives and co-workers who are not Christians. What are their views on religion? Christianity? God?
2. Visualise Christian directors. Make it a point to ask for their personal testimonies. Specifically: When did they become Christians? Why? Who witnessed to them? How?
3. Review Saul's conversion to Paul (Acts 9:1–31).
4. What do your unsaved directors have in common with *Saul*?
5. What do your Christian directors have in common with *Paul*?
6. Use your imagination to consider how Saul would have responded to an alternate approach from God.

8

Witnessing to the Entertainer

'If God deals in averages, I'll make it,' is the heartfelt belief of the entertainer. Another version of the same sentiment is, 'I'm no worse than any of my friends, so I'll just take my chances.'

Since entertainers live for the fun in life, the last thing they want to do is replace it with what they see as the dreary lifestyle of Christianity. Even those entertainers who have never opened a Bible know that the 'pretty good' lifestyles they lead are not pristine and that they would be required to give up 'the good life'. Unfortunately, they cannot imagine the abundant life of love and joy that Jesus Christ offers.

I asked Amy, an entertainer colleague, why she isn't a Christian. She said, 'My philosophy at school and college was to run wild and have a good time. I never thought beyond the moment. Frankly, because of what I did to my body – I smoked too much and I drank too much – I never really thought I'd make it to my thirtieth birthday. Now, a year and a half from my fortieth birthday, I am starting to rethink the ambivalent, almost nonattitude I have had about God and about Jesus Christ.'

The best way I have found to reach Amy is to follow the line in the popular hymn, 'They will know we are Christians by our love.' That love has gradually taken shape during the past five years as we have operated competing portrait photography businesses less than one mile apart in a town of twenty-eight thousand.

My story with Amy actually began five years before I met her, when my husband and I first hung out our sign and opened our studio. There was one main photographic studio in town and another that was edging towards the retirement phase. We had been photographing weddings on a freelance basis, and in 1983 we decided to take the plunge and begin operating full time.

The day the new phone book arrived, my heart raced as I flipped to our listing. When I saw 'Boursier Photography' in print, I felt we had arrived. It didn't take long for the bubble to burst.

During the next year, we were the subject of much idle gossip. None of it was complimentary. None of it was pleasant. All of it was generated by a studio owner who felt unrealistically threatened by a new name in the phone book. It took every ounce of faith and love to not pay back evil for evil, but we turned the painful issue over to God. That's where Amy entered the picture.

When we moved from a residential home studio to a full-service studio in a commercial office complex in October 1987, we couldn't wait to place the ad in the Yellow Pages the following spring. Again we eagerly opened the phone book – only to find that there was another new listing. Amy!

I immediately picked up the phone and invited her to join the Professional Photographers of Cape Cod. It was almost déjà vu, because our direct competitor when we first opened was president of the Cape Cod photographers' group. (He had deliberately not invited us to join.) Now I was president with a new studio to extend an invitation to.

During the intervening years I have let Amy sit in on classes I taught on posing and lighting and sales and marketing, even though her business is only a few streets away. I've also helped to pave the way and get her involved in various professional photography organisations.

The photographer who treated Mike and me poorly when we first opened gave Amy exactly the same treatment. My genuine concern about her personal and business life is so striking in contrast that she couldn't possibly miss it. As a result, Amy has been open to hear about the difference in my life, and I've told her I owe it to Jesus Christ.

Peer Pressure

The entertainer invented the term 'peer pressure'. In the words of my teenage entertainer son, Jason, 'My friends are my life!' Everything entertainers say and do and wear is to please their friends. Before entertainers make commitments to Christ, they consider whether the decision will cause their friends to no longer like them. Your job could be to help the entertainers take a good look at their 'friends' and help them decide whether or not they have their priorities in the right order.

Entertainer John is a perfect example of getting priorities mixed up. The middle child of a large family, he was left to fend for himself when his parents split up during his early teenage years. Typical of many of his siblings, he turned to alcohol. He dropped out of school at seventeen to marry his girlfriend, who was five months pregnant.

The newlyweds left their home town and headed to a seaside area, where John teamed up with his brothers in the building industry. When they had a contract on the nearby island, they had to take a ferry over and back each day. John and the boys would see who could drink the most during the forty-five-minute ride at the end of the day. Needless to say, his wife had to haul him home when the boat docked. He also frequently went drinking with the lads in the evening, and it was not uncommon for his wife to have a stranger open her front door and unceremoniously drop John across the threshold.

Fear finally broke through the peer pressure. 'My cousin came to work with us,' John says, 'and he hammered me every day about becoming a Christian. I told him to knock it off, but he kept after me day after day, from April to October.

'Right when his job was almost over, I cut my arm. My cousin stayed on through the winter to drive me and help me at the job sites. Finally, a week before he left the job, he gave me *The Late Great Planet Earth* and asked me to read it. I read the book just to shut him up. I came to Christ because of fear. That's not the reason now, but in the beginning that was definitely the reason.'

Saving face with peers might not be a need for directors, but to entertainers it's paramount. A family friend who is an off-the-top-of-the-charts entertainer loves to tell the story of how he was poorly treated by a rural church where he had been active in music ministry. (In true entertainer style, he has told the story in minute detail so many times that I stopped listening long ago.) The shabby treatment he received caused him to lose faith in the church. Except for the occasional wedding or Christmas service, he hasn't been back in fifteen years. He can't get over his hurt feelings of all those years ago.

As a logical-minded director who doesn't have the entertainer need to save face with peers or to have piles of close personal friends, I tried using a matter-of-fact approach to his reason for giving up on God. I told him that Christ wasn't acting through those people and that Christ is the reason we go to church. I asked him not to let the poor actions of others stand between him and God.

Logic may mobilise a director to action, but it doesn't move an entertainer. You can use every reason in the book, but the entertainer, who operates at the *emotional* level, just won't hear you. The closest I came to penetrating my friend's emotions was to point out that his decision not to return to church no longer affects only his salvation but now has an impact on his family's spiritual commitment as well. His young son, who was a toddler when my friend stopped attending church, is at college now, and his daughters weren't even born when the church incident happened. I pointed out that by taking no action he was, in reality, shaping his children's destiny. (His son provided tangible evidence of this when he recently told me that the only god he acknowledges is the sun god.)

I would love to write that the family now walks arm in arm down the aisle of the sanctuary every Sunday morning, but that is not the case. My friend blew the dust off the guitar he hadn't played in more than a decade, his wife attends church once again, and the topic of 'religion' no longer has the sting it once had. The issue of yielding the will over to God remains unsettled, but the chapter is not closed. Their story reminds us that our responsibility is to pray and witness; only the Holy Spirit can do the convicting.

Last-Ditch Objection

In the world of sales the final objection a prospective client throws out to keep from buying a product is called the 'last-ditch objection'. The sceptical entertainer's final excuse is often 'What about the people who have never heard about

God or Jesus Christ?' Entertainers reckon they will slide in under the wire with the ones who have never heard the message. After all, they think they can't be any worse than *them*! Romans 1:18–20 says,

> The wrath of God is being revealed from heaven against all the godlessness and wickedness of men who suppress the truth by their wickedness, since what may be known about God is plain to them, because God has made it plain to them. For since the creation of the world God's invisible qualities – his eternal power and divine nature – have been clearly seen, being understood from what has been made, so that men are without excuse.

While directors rely on their good works, entertainers expect their 'pretty good' nature to get them through the gate. The answer is to help the entertainer see that no one will be condemned for not hearing about Jesus but for violating their own moral standards. Paul writes about this issue in Romans 2:12–13: 'He will punish sin wherever it is found. He will punish the heathen when they sin, even though they never had God's written laws, for down in their hearts they know right from wrong. God's laws are written within them; their own conscience accuses them, or sometimes excuses them' (LB).

Overcoming Excuses

With all of these excuses in mind, your best bet when witnessing to an entertainer is to keep the discussion light and fun. Avoid arguing and don't get preachy. Remember that entertainers thrive on being the centre of attention. Find out as much as you can about their concerns by allowing them plenty of time to talk. Keep your discussion bold and open, and stay away from too many details.

After you have had a chance to listen to their story, personalise your witness by giving testimonials about other Christians who were in a similar situation. You will be even more effective if you can put the story into the first person. For example, 'I was worried about what my friends at work would say too. I finally decided it was a decision that ultimately I would be held responsible for. All my worrying proved unnecessary! Since my friends like and respect me for who I am, they easily accepted and respected my decision to become a Christian.'

Simple acts of kindness are also great ways to get through to the friendly, spontaneous nature of the entertainer. In our hectic world with everyone racing from home to work to school to home and back again, the simplest gestures of kindness will set you apart from the masses. Through the years I have tried both bolting through life and slowing down to enjoy it. No one benefits when I race through the day, but everyone notices when I get off the treadmill and offer a few kindnesses. The gesture can be as simple as offering a jug of water.

I remember pushing my then six-month-old son around the block in a push-chair on a hot July afternoon. A young family was moving in up the street, and sweat was pouring off the workers as they struggled to get all the heavy furniture out of the van and up the steep hill that led to the front steps. I knew I wasn't furniture-moving material, but I wanted to do something to help. I pushed Jason home, filled a big red plastic jug with cold water and brought it back up the street.

That simple act of hospitality broke the ice, and my new neighbours and I gradually established strong ties that have endured through many years and many moves. Terry later told me she and her husband just couldn't believe this strange lady would bring them a jug of cold water.

Part of the shock value for this little act stems from the fact that people in our area are not known for being neighbourly. A minister was pointing out this unfriendliness by joking that it took him ten years to get to know the names of the people living just next door. After the laughter subsided, he admitted he had exaggerated: it took only eight years. Heads were nodding in agreement during the ripple of laughter that followed!

Getting through and establishing a relationship is an ideal beginning for witnessing to the people-person entertainer, and the first step is to get out there and meet your neighbours! Robert L. Burgess said,

> Relationships are real important. They need to have a sense of acceptance and fellowship. You can reach them on a more emotional level, and continual contact is important to them. Look at the apostle Peter. He needed the significant emotional event of denial and then Jesus coming back and speaking to him three times. It was *love* that brought Peter back to Jesus, not authority.

Linda, an art teacher, explains her wobbly walk to find Christ. 'I grew up with very little church. I went to Sunday school when I was ten, eleven and twelve, but my family didn't encourage or support me at all. When it came time to be married, I would have been quite happy with a registrar, but my fiancé insisted on a minister. Once we were married, I started attending church with my husband.

'The church had a very large and very active choir. It was the music that finally reached me. I can't sit there and read and be intellectual about religion, but I feel God's presence through the music. Being in church for the music makes me want to listen and learn the rest.'

Singing with the choir touches two aspects of the entertainer personality. The music touches the sensual side of her personality, while choir practice provides a social outlet and peer group.

Typical of an entertainer, Linda relates her faith and her church attendance to her senses. 'I feel pretty disgusting after a week in the world, what with fighting with my spouse or the hassles at work. An hour in God's house during the Sunday worship seems to clean me out and give me a fresh start for the week.'

The very way entertainers witness is a clue to how their unsaved peers would relate. Their inborn gift of the gab and ease with people make personal evangelism a natural style. Where others struggle to have the courage to walk up to strangers or keep a conversation going for more than a tenth of a second, entertainers have the wind to go the distance. They are also good at telling funny stories about their walks with the Lord.

'When others witness to me, it is their uplifting nature that inspires me,' explained an entertainer who goes to my church. 'They are positive people who look for the good in life. I see their dedicated faith and want to be just like them.'

David, an entertainer, said he has been inspired to witness by watching other Christians share their faith out of love for Christ and love for people. Typical of many entertainers, he sees the message of Jesus Christ as being all about love. More technical-minded personalities might find his faith naive, theologically weak or even manipulative. However, when you hear his gentle voice and see his eyes light up when he talks about what a difference Jesus Christ has made in his life, you almost envy him the depth of love for the Lord and the degree of commitment to witnessing that he obviously has.

'When it comes from love, you cannot offend anyone in any faith,' David said. 'I try to make my message all benefit. I get my listeners to see what I have and then try to make them want it too. I give the message "Isn't this wonderful?" I talk about all the good stuff and then tell them they can have it too.'

Witnessing to the Entertainer Round-Up Questions

1. Visualise the unsaved entertainers in your life. What are their views on religion? Christianity? God?
2. Visualise the Christian entertainers you know. Ask one or two when and why they became Christians. Also ask what or who influenced them to become or continue being Christians.
3. Read about David (1 Sam. 17:26–37; 2 Sam. 6:12–16, 21–22; 11:1–27.
4. Compare the entertainer strengths and weaknesses between David the humble shepherd and King David the successful leader and warrior.
5. Read about the difference faith in God made in King David's response to his entertainer weaknesses (Ps. 51:1–19).
6. What do your unsaved entertainer friends have in common with David?
7. What do your Christian friends have in common with David?
8. How can you help bridge this gap?

9

Witnessing to the Peacekeeper

It almost seems appropriate to begin this chapter about peacekeepers with a blank paragraph or two. It's not that people with this quiet personality have nothing interesting to say, it's that they don't willingly offer to say it. Whenever I have given a lecture or workshop on witnessing, I always invite the audience to share their stories with me. To keep it as non-threatening as possible, I ask them to leave their names and phone numbers and a suggested time for a short telephone interview. Half a dozen people usually respond. I have yet to have a peacekeeper volunteer! The only way I got stories about this quiet-natured personality for this book was to find the stories myself.

When you witness to a peacekeeper, you will find the same struggles I had in conducting the interviews. Simply put, change is too much trouble for this soft-spoken, pleasant, gracious and calm person whose number one fear is conflict of any kind. Peacekeepers would much rather stick with the status quo for ever than rethink their positions and possibly make changes.

The witnessing challenge is to help the peacekeeper understand that 'without faith it is impossible to please God, because anyone who comes to him must believe that he exists and that he rewards those who earnestly seek him' (Heb. 11:6). Earnest seeking is not a passive activity. It requires more than a feeling. It requires action.

Feelings for Family

Peacekeepers have the highest family values of all the personalities. Scripture verses and Christian teaching about children, marriage and relationships will have the greatest impact with them.

Russ, a peacekeeper, talks about how family values brought him back to church and to Christ. 'When I was small, my mother brought me to church. I was an acolyte, and I was very involved in Sunday school and youth group. I threw it all up when I became a teenager simply because I no longer *had* to go.

'When my children were born, my mother started nudging me back to church by making gentle comments here and there. Then, when my sons got involved in the Scouts, with their promise to serve God, I got involved again with the church. I didn't know anything about any other religion, but I did know Christianity from my youth. It is the best thing there is, and I wanted my sons to grow up with Christ.'

Family values also finally made peacekeeper Roberta 'get off the fence', as she put it, and make a commitment to her faith. She was brought up in a Methodist church but switched to Presbyterian when she got married. 'My husband's faith was much more important to him at that time than my faith was to me, so we decided to bring up our children in his church.'

After fifteen years of marriage and two primary-age children, Roberta finally took steps to join her husband's church. 'My children were asking questions about why I didn't go to the same church. I would explain that I was a member of another church. After enough of those questions, I decided it was time to get off the fence and live my faith. I knew I had to either begin attending my church regularly or officially join and attend my husband's church.'

Fear of conflict keeps a lot of quiet Christians home on Sunday mornings. Susan grew up with a strong Christian faith. When she married a man who was ambivalent, it was easier to let Sunday services come and go unnoticed than to take a stand for her faith. As with Russ, it took the priority of children and her responsibility to them to motivate her to come home to God.

Taking a Cue from a Gentle Heart

Your witness to a peacekeeper must be non-threatening, sincere and gentle. Of all the personalities, the peacekeeper generally takes the longest to sift and process information, so you need to keep the pace slow and conversational. Trust, friendship and credibility are important, and peacekeepers are ideal candidates for one-to-one evangelism. Take time to find out about their feelings, and plan to give them lots of reassurance and nurturing.

Not only do you need to establish your genuine concern for the peacekeeper, you need to be concerned about the peacekeeper's family as well. I was once pulled up short by a long-time friend for not asking after her mother, who had had an operation the year before. It wasn't that I didn't care. It just never occurred to me to ask! I had no idea I was insulting my friend by not asking, because if the roles were reversed, I wouldn't care if she didn't ask about the members of my family whom she hardly knew. Since so many of my friends are peacekeepers, I keep consciously trying to remember this lesson.

Mark, a Methodist minister, offers these suggestions for friendship evangelism, an ideal way to reach peacekeepers. 'First, you must be conformed to the image of Christ because who you are is what your witness is.

'Second, you must meet people where they are, on their own terms, without any presuppositions. Form a relationship before you begin to talk about religion *per se*. You must accept the person and show that you care for him. Then, when you do witness, his first response will be to trust you because you have accepted him.

'Third, you must know when to talk about religion and when not to. You can't force the issue. Your witness needs to be a response to his need. You must meet people where they are and not the other way round.'

Jim Petersen writes about the problem with witnessing to friends at work and school in his book *Living Proof*. Although these people may be our friends both socially and intellectually, when we don't take enough time to establish rapport before we share the gospel, we are stepping on their toes. It's unfair, he says, to talk about a message this personal without first 'bonding' the friendship on a personal level. This is never more true than with the relationship-oriented peacekeeper. Petersen writes, 'Efforts at evangelism are often either an unannounced assault on a stranger, or little more than being nice to someone.'

Part of establishing this rapport comes with slowing down and allowing for two-way communication. Instead of saying what you want to say and moving right along, you need to get the peacekeeper involved in the conversation. The only way you're going to do this is to ask questions and keep your mouth shut long enough for the peacekeeper to process the question, come up with an answer and formulate a reply. If you're an outspoken entertainer or an impatient director, the time lapse between your question and the peacekeeper's reply can seem a millennium!

If you have to bite your tongue until it bleeds, do it. Silence keeps you from saying more than you need to, and it makes the other person talk. If you ask a question such as 'What do you think a "real" Christian is like?' or 'What is your perception of God?' and you don't like (or receive) the answer, just sit tight. If you keep your mouth closed, the silence lets the other person know you want to hear more. Don't think of your silence as forcing peacekeepers to talk so much as allowing them time to think.

Years ago, a commander was transferred to an army fort on the American frontier. It wasn't long before he was at a peace talk with an important Indian chief. Working through a translator, he nervously asked the chief a few questions. The commander was surprised when he didn't get any reply. After the meeting he asked the translator what went wrong. 'That is what we call "Indian time",' said the translator. 'He has enough respect for your questions to go away and think about them before answering.' All the commander needed was some patience (from Michael P. Green, ed., *Illustrations for Biblical Preaching* [Grand Rapids, Mich.: Baker Book House, 1982], p. 223).

A Peacekeeper's Search

Peter, a cancer-research physicist and an associate professor of experimental pathology, is a peacekeeper-analyser who embarked on a slow, steady, meticulous quest for the truth of Jesus Christ. Born in Wales and raised as a member of the Church of England, Peter said, 'I don't think I ever became really *not* a Christian, in the sense that in times of need I would pray to Jesus. That was something I always fell back on. But I began to question things that the Church taught. I was taught, for example, that if you didn't have the chance to become a Christian in this life, if you grew up in a jungle or were a Buddhist, then you would go to hell. I couldn't believe that a God who was so compassionate to come to this earth to die for us would be so cruel as to just let the people go to hell because they didn't know about Jesus.' Doubt in that teaching set Peter off on a quest for the perfect religion.

'I was always into science, and I had always felt things could and should be tested. I suppose I began to apply my scientific approach to my faith. I went to a class in comparative religions, I became very interested in Eastern religions, and I studied different "natural philosophies". I found that a basic principle ran through all the religions. That element is almost indescribable, but basically it was an element of God.

'The problem was it was not a personal element. It was all philosophical. I had put aside the things I'd been taught in my Christian faith because of the man-made rules we had added. Then I came to the painful realisation that I'd replaced Christian principles, which were personal, with this new idol that was impersonal. It created an unhappy state for me.

'During all this time, when I was down, I would always pray to Jesus to show me the right religion. It was almost like I was a small boy being naughty in the garden and then I got scared and ran back inside the house.'

Peter figuratively came back inside for good when he revisited a lake in England where he had spent holidays as a child, and realised that in many peaceful visits there he had experienced grace. When he went to the nearby All Saints Church to pray, he came to the firm realisation that Jesus Christ helped all the saints through time and that he was helping Peter find his lost faith.

'I realised that Jesus shows himself to everyone who has a clean heart and who seeks the truth,' says Peter. 'When I was in the church, I heard a voice say to me, "Now you must keep the faith." I knew that meant I was to stop sorting through all of this and stop asking for physical demonstrations. I knew Jesus Christ was there for me and that he loved me. I went away with a quiet but firm faith. "Seek and ye shall find."'

The people who witnessed to this gentle scientist during his years of seeking were consistent, but low-key. 'Nothing profound was said, but the right person always seemed to be saying the right thing at the right time,' Peter says. 'It could have been as simple as someone mentioning they were going to church on Sunday morning, but it was the little bit I needed to remind me of church and of Jesus calling me there.'

Subtle Touches, Quiet Witnessing

The tender words and subtle touches Peter felt are needed everywhere, and particularly by peacekeepers. You've heard it said that for all the millions of people who go to bed hungry for food each night, at least that many more are starving for a little love and attention. We can send our financial support to Africa and Asia to buy food, but we do not need to look for spectacular ways to love the lonely. Opportunities abound for doing good in the day-to-day activities of our lives.

As one soft-spoken member of my church said, 'We can

spread Christ's love by our actions. Just by spreading little words here and there, you can share your faith more than you realise.'

A twenty-year-old student explained that he sees witnessing as both verbal and non-verbal. The non-verbal may mean being there for a friend, showing that you are ready to listen when they need to talk. Peter, for example, had a conversation with a fellow university student just before the Christmas vacation. 'She was telling me how it really didn't feel much like Christmas to her and she asked how my Christmas was going. I told her it was going just fine because of what Christmas means to me. I hadn't planned to give her a sermon, but when she pressed me for more information, I told her I look at Christmas as a celebration of Christ's birth. Because I was willing to listen to her, she was willing to listen to me.'

We'll do better to present the love and joy and relationship elements of Jesus Christ to a peacekeeper than to promote church activities, Christian morals and how much enjoyment we get from our devotional life. The former relates to the values the peacekeeper holds so dear, and the latter simply sounds like too much work!

Nicely Naive

One downfall of peacekeepers is to be nicely naive. That means they can be drawn into false doctrine more easily than any other personality. This may be because digging below a surface presentation takes more work than they want to tackle or because taking an easier route (away from biblical doctrine) requires little discipline. Obviously all people who do not believe in Jesus Christ as Lord and Saviour hold to one false doctrine or another. Peacekeepers are so pleasant in how they talk about their false doctrines that they can bait you – without your realising it – with 'well-meaning' questions they have no real desire for you to answer.

I learned my lesson on this, as usual, the hard way. When Operation Desert Storm was launched a few years ago, I found myself embroiled in a personal battle with a customer who was among the 5 per cent of Americans against the war. She pleasantly loaded her guns and pointed them right at me by asking if I thought it was God's will that the war took place.

Since this woman knew I had been spending a lot of time studying the Bible, I foolishly thought she wanted my honest opinion. I said I didn't think God was probably doing back flips over the evils of Saddam Hussein's actions and that war has been part of the choice humans have always made. Instead of being able to witness to her about the love, joy and peace of Jesus Christ, I ended up in a long-winded, long-running debate over the rights and wrongs of war.

In the middle of all this, I came across Proverbs 26:4–5: 'Do not answer a fool according to his folly, or you will be like him yourself.' In other words, don't play into someone's trap by giving your honest reply to her loaded question! If someone is trying to bait you into an argument, sidestep the issue or let it go.

When I replayed the experience in my mind, I couldn't believe how obvious it was that there was no right answer and that she really didn't want to hear what the Bible had to say anyway. Her pleasant, naive attitude had duped me. What I originally thought was a chance to talk about the love Jesus brings to the world ended up a debate about the human response – war – to deal with the evils of the world.

Too Much Trouble

The final objection peacekeepers make will remain unvoiced but ever-present. This is their own inertia. When peacekeepers glimpse all the daily changes involved in being a Christian, they may choose the way of less resistance and continue in their false beliefs.

To help them over their hurdle, first explain that no magic *x* amount of faith is required of them. In Matthew 17:20 Jesus says, 'If you have faith as small as a mustard seed, you can say to this mountain, "Move from here to there" and it will move. Nothing will be impossible for you.'

Next, use examples in the peacekeeper's daily life that show faith in action. Flipping on a light switch, for example, requires faith, because we expect the lights to come on even though we may not know how the process actually works. 'Faith is being sure of what we hope for and certain of what we do not see' (Heb. 11:1).

Finally, we need to encourage passive peacekeepers not to sit and wait for faith to fall into their laps. 'Everyone who *calls* on the name of the Lord will be saved' (Rom. 10:13). We need to put our own faith into action, show them the value of a close, personal relationship with the Lord, and persistently encourage them to call on him.

Witnessing to the Peacekeeper Round-Up Questions

1. Visualise the unsaved peacekeepers in your life. What are their views on religion? Christianity? God?
2. Visualise the Christian peacekeepers you know. Ask one or two when and why they become Christians. Ask what or who influenced them to become or continue to be Christians.
3. Review the story of Eli (1 Sam. 3:10–15; 4:12–22).

4. Read about Mary, the mother of Jesus (Luke 1:26–38; 2:1–19).
5. What do your peacekeepers have in common with the priest? with Mary?
6. How can you help peacekeepers bridge the gap between idle curiosity about faith or passivity (Eli) and quietly accepting the Lord and following his commandments (Mary)?

10

Witnessing to the Analyser

The cautious, conservative and introverted analyser is sceptical by nature and likely to think that 'faith' in Jesus Christ is believing in something that isn't true. When analysers say they have 'intellectual problems' with Christianity, they are not just fobbing you off with a smoke screen. They sincerely mean it.

When you witness to analysers, plan to have your facts straight. They will need a lot of supporting data complete with cross-references. If you give a personal testimony, plan to back it up with solid, factual, tangible evidence. To them, faith must be founded on more than a feeling. Not only do analysers require more data, they take longer to process the information. Your approach must be logical, and you need to allow the analyser enough time to think things through.

John, an undergraduate, says he has always been impressed by Christians who have challenged him to look for the answers on his own. He talked about a professor in charge of such campus activities as organising Bible studies and student ministries. John said, 'When you are talking to him, he challenges you to come up with why you do what you do and why you believe what you believe. He always has his own answer, but he gets you to come up with yours.

I admire him for his ability to do this so it is not condescending.'

Nothing turns off analysers more quickly than condescension. Because of their quest for excellence, analysers tend to be more highly educated than everyone else, and they pride themselves on their knowledge. The last thing they want is a know-it-all Christian telling them just how much they don't know. Or, as an analyser friend recently said, 'I hate it when other people think they know what is best for me . . . about anything!'

Analyser John suggests simply asking what the person *doesn't* believe. 'It might be that they were involved in a church and something went wrong, or they might never have heard the message before. You need to know where they are coming from as much as they need to know where you are coming from.'

A good starting point for discussion is the concept of faith itself. How do you explain faith in analyser terms? With the gadgets and gizmos they love, of course. Technology is continually introducing new consumer doodahs that we purchase and use in complete faith. Each time I send an invisible message through the telephone wires by the fax machine, I am amazed. I have no clue how it works. All I know is that I put the piece of paper face down, dial the number, push start, and in seconds the machine sends a full page of type, or even a photograph, halfway around the world to our photographer friends in New Zealand. I can't see the bits and bytes travelling through the wires, and I have never been able to grasp the particulars of how it works, but I do know the fax works, because my friends always fax back.

Faith in God works in a similar fashion. You don't see the physical being of God, but you see what he does in the world around us. Peacekeeper Peter, the cancer-research scientist, has a simple way to show God at work to his sceptical friends. 'All my scientist peers know I am a Christian, and often we talk "philosophy". I realise that most of the people who ask me questions might mask their real questions, but I do know they realise that they have a piece missing in their lives.

'The problem is they can't see beyond the microscopes they use all day. The solution might be as simple as walking on the beach at night and pointing to the stars. They suddenly see how insignificant they are and how impossible it is for them to solve everything. They realise that they don't have to solve the world's problems because who or what is already sustaining the stars and everything else is doing a good job.' He adds, 'I've done this several times, and people usually respond with tears because they are so relieved. For many that is the first peace they have had about their worries for years.'

An Intellectual Appeal

Looking at the stars or hearing a story about faith in a fax machine is barely the beginning of the 'proof' you will need to present to the pessimistic, worst-case-scenario thinker/analyser. An intellectual appeal to investigate the facts about Jesus Christ is the answer. To motivate analysers to listen, you should appeal to their strong desire for accuracy. Ask how much research they have done on the historical person of Jesus Christ, or how much study of the Bible strictly from a literary perspective. Find out whether they have systematically weighed the pros and cons of Christianity. Most likely, they haven't done any of this. If that is the case, motivate them to find their own answers while offering to serve as a research assistant. You may not be able to completely *prove* Christianity is true, but you can help the analyser find some pretty good reasons that it *ought* to be true.

How the analyser sees your faith in action is going to be a large part of your credibility as an assistant to this sceptic. Unless we are fully persuaded in our own minds that Jesus is the Christ and the Bible is the Word of God, we won't be able to fully communicate and 'prove' the gospel to the analyser. If all you can answer is 'Just because' when someone asks why you believe, you're not going to be any use helping analysers discover their own faith.

It's only half of the story when we sing, 'You ask me how I know he lives. He lives within my heart.' An internal feeling won't impress the typical analyser. That's why 1 Peter 3:15 calls us to stand ready to defend our faith. As author and speaker Charles E. Jones says, 'A person ought to know what he believes, why he believes it, and then *believe* it!'

Analyser John says that not knowing why is a common problem among his peers at a Christian college in America. 'It was the hardest thing for me to find the "why". The only reason I used to give for "why" was that I grew up in the Church. Even as I was saying it, I knew that wasn't enough.

'Gradually I became aware of other reasons why I believe. I did this by going to other churches and looking for the answers on my own. I was always confident in what I believed, but I wanted and needed to know the "why". It was a slow, progressive process, but eventually I was able to say, "This is what I believe, and this is why." If you can figure out *why* you believe, you will have much more validity in your witnessing.' Particularly to an analyser.

Not everyone, and not every analyser, will come up with the same answer to "why". As my cancer-research friend

Peter said, 'We don't all have the same questions, so the answers we find are naturally going to be different.'

The answer an analyser minister found was faith in scholars who had lived long before him. He was working on his doctorate when he realised that the answers he was seeking were becoming more important than his actual relationship to Jesus Christ. 'I came to realise that men far cleverer and far more educated than I had accepted Christ as real. I trust the knowledge of men like St Augustine and Aquinas on so many other things. I decided to trust them on their faith in Jesus Christ as well.'

The minister, like many other analysers, found faith in the history books.

Historical Proof

First, establish the fact that Jesus is a historical figure who lived and breathed. Your sceptical analyser will find volumes of books about Jesus as a teacher, prophet and rabbi. His story is not exclusive to the New Testament.

Once the analyser finds Jesus in the history books, the next step is to establish him as the Christ. As Paul said, 'If Christ has not been raised, our preaching is useless and so is your faith' (1 Cor. 15:14). Since the cornerstone of the Christian faith is the resurrection, you need to lay out the substantiating facts.

Early sermons did not attempt to persuade people to believe the tomb was empty. This was considered common knowledge. Plenty of people had seen the risen Christ, including a group of more than five hundred people. In 1 Corinthians 15 Paul reminded his audience that these people were still alive and could confirm Christ's resurrection.

The very existence of the Christian Church is another

historical fact substantiating Christ and Christianity. The Church dates back to around AD 32 Palestine, where the only socially accepted religion was Judaism. When Jesus was taken from the Garden of Gethsemane, his disciples fled in panic. Their association with a 'criminal' would not hold them in good graces with either their fellow Jews or the Romans. In fact, Peter deliberately denied he knew Jesus three times between the evening arrest and the following sunrise.

What could later cause this handful of beaten men to have the temerity to break with the strong social and religious norms of the day? Consider Peter. The same scared man who cowardly denied that he knew Christ risked his life forty days later at Pentecost to preach about Jesus. Ask the analyser what could cause this about-face.

The proof doesn't end at Pentecost. All the disciples faced the test of torture and martyrdom for their testimony and faith in Jesus Christ. All the apostles had to do was deny Christ, but they chose to die instead. People will die for what they believe to be true, even though it may really be false. But no one will deliberately die for something they know is fake. Ask the analyser if he or she would die for a lie.

Gamaliel, a Pharisee and expert on religious law during the time of Christ, was one of the first officials to defend the teachings of the early Christians. He advised the religious council to leave the Christian leaders alone, saying, 'If their purpose or activity is of human origin, it will fail. But if it is from God, you will not be able to stop these men; you will only find yourselves fighting against God' (Acts 5:34–42).

The fact that the New Testament survived is another credential supporting the validity of Christianity. Martin Luther once observed,

> Mighty potentates have raged against this book and sought to destroy and uproot it – Alexander the Great and princes of Egypt and Babylon, the monarchs of Persia, of Greece, and of Rome, the emperors Julius and Augustus – but they prevailed nothing. They are gone while the book remains, and it will remain forever and forever, perfect and entire as it was declared at first. Who has thus helped it – who protected it against such mighty forces? Not me, surely, but God Himself who is master of all things.

Sunday worship and the celebration of the Last Supper also back up the fact of the resurrection. The sabbath had been observed on Saturday among God's people since God had created heaven and earth. It was faithfully observed by all Jews, including the disciples. 'By the seventh day [Saturday] God had finished the work he had been doing; so on the seventh day he rested from all his work. And God blessed the seventh day and made it holy, because on it he rested from all the work of creating that he had done' (Gen. 2:2–3). Ask the analyser how easily you would break an age-old tradition that everyone you knew and respected continued to observe.

The Last Supper is a similar testament to the empty tomb. It did not become a morbid ritual in memory of death but a celebration of the sacrifice Jesus made for us. It is done in honour of his life and resurrection.

For contemporary proof, look to the thousands now living who bear testimony of lives changed by Christ. He has done in these people exactly what he said he would do. Ask the analyser how it is possible for so many people, through so many centuries, to be deceived.

Giving In

Where directors struggle to relinquish control of their lives, and entertainers worry about losing fun and friends, and peacekeepers dislike the effort Christianity involves, analysers worry about looking stupid. They don't want to make a decision for Christ until they have ploughed through mountains of research and *know* they are making the best possible choice. The basic issue is simply giving in to God.

Jo, a retired shopkeeper, explains that she finally 'gave in' to God. Although she had attended church all her life, she had never really heard the Word. 'I was married and had two small children, a home and a successful business. But something was missing. I would look out of my picture window and just cry.'

Jo had a new baby-sitter who always brought tracts, which were filed in the bin. But Jo says, 'I began to wonder if what the tracts were saying was really in the Bible, so I blew the dust off our family Bible and began cross-referencing the tracts. This went on for a year or so. Meanwhile, the sitter asked if she could take my three- and four-year-old kids to holiday Bible club.

'At the end of the second week the parents were invited to come and hear their little darlings recite verses and sing their songs. It was the first time I realised that a whole church actually believed this stuff.' A few months later Jo accepted Christ.

'I'm a very investigative person,' she says, 'and it was very hard to accept anything by faith. What is faith? What button do you push? Show me what faith looks like. The proof for me was seeing a whole church full of people who were there to *worship*. There was a love and a fellowship that I had never seen or felt before. You could see it, and you could feel it.' She saw the proof, so she found her faith.

Witnessing to the Analyser Round-Up Questions

1. Visualise the unsaved analysers in your life. What are their views on religion? Christianity? God?
2. Visualise the Christian analysers in your life. Ask them why they became Christians. Ask who and what influenced them to become or stay a Christian.
3. Review the story of Thomas (John 11:16; 14:1–7; 20:24–29).
4. Read about Moses (Exod. 4:29–31; 5:1–3; 6:1–13; 8:1–2; 9:1–4; 10:1–6; 11:1–6).
5. What do the analysers you know have in common with Thomas? Moses?
6. How can you help to bridge the gap between the doubt typical of the analyser and the steadfast faith that enabled Moses to go back to Pharaoh again and again?
7. Read a basic book on why you believe (facts that support the reality of Jesus Christ and the resurrection) so you are prepared to answer the many questions you will encounter from analysers.

11

Getting into Step with Your Style

'Go and make disciples of all nations, baptising them in the name of the Father and of the Son and of the Holy Spirit, and teaching them to obey everything I have commanded you. And surely I am with you always, to the very end of the age' (Matt. 28:19–20).

Surveys and statistics are part of the Western way of life. You can find facts, figures and percentages on everything – including evangelism. It has been estimated that only four out of a hundred Christians know how to communicate the gospel. Of those, only one out of ten actually uses that know-how to witness. That means that only 1 to 4 per cent of Western Christians take on the responsibility of evangelism. It is not a case of the extroverts versus the introverts. With the percentage estimate so low, clearly all four personality profiles are shirking their duties.

Since you are reading a book on witnessing, you obviously *want* to share your faith more effectively. But I can't assume also that you necessarily *like* to witness. You may have picked this book for the same reason I always buy the newest books on managing finances and handling simple investments. I hate the nit-picking details of personal finance, but I keep hoping that something from the books will rub off on me!

Take It like a Soldier

One titbit I hope you get from this book is *learning not to duck daily witnessing opportunities* – your faith is on the firing range, and this is your chance to squarely defend it. Consider all the primary conversation topics that come up every day: work, religion, politics, taxes, moral issues, relationships, hobbies. All these topics can be natural openings for us to relate our stance, which, backed up by prior Bible study and prayer, will accurately reflect Christ's own.

Allow no room for grey areas in your stance: we are either for Christ or against him. Either we believe in him and his teachings wholeheartedly or we don't. This sounded too simplistic to me until I looked at the issue from the perspective of an unbeliever.

When I was home with the flu one afternoon a few years ago, mindlessly flipping stations on the television, I caught the tail end of a chat show dealing with Christianity and witnessing. The guest was relating a conversation with an ardent atheist whom he had visited on his deathbed. The atheist told the visiting Christian he had long ago discounted Christianity because, if it were true, he said, 'I would crawl on my hands and knees across a bed of nails to do anything for Christ. I do not see such devotion in his followers.'

I felt as if I'd been slapped in the face! Although I have long since forgotten the details of the programme, I hope I always remember that atheist's stinging comment – because it is true.

Everyone Has a Style That Works

Our personality differences are important elements of our witnessing. These factors give us our style. The wider the variety of styles, the wider the reach we have for Christ.

Robert L. Burgess, a trainer for the Personal Profile System, explains how God used four different styles with the apostles.

> [Directors'] style tends to be direct and sometimes more confrontational . . . They tend to be weak on the area of acceptance of others. Paul was a [director] – he confronted people. A [director] can confront another [director] because they talk on the same wave length, but that same style might frighten a [peacekeeper] away.
>
> A [peacekeeper] will get along very well with another [peacekeeper] because they will both be relationship builders. So many times the [peacekeeper] doesn't believe he has the charismatic ability to convince anyone to be a Christian, but he does build the relationship strongly. That becomes the witness. The apostle John was always the one who had the strong relationship with Jesus. John, the quiet one, did his greatest work alone, on the Island of Patmos, writing the book of Revelation.
>
> The [entertainer] has the gift of being a good talker. Peter's greatest strength was his ability to talk to a crowd. People were drawn to him. Meanwhile, the [entertainer] is typically poor on relationship building, and Peter was ultimately challenged in the area of relationship. Peter's popularity was important. He was torn between his own need to be needed and loved and liked, but he also loved Jesus. When he was confronted to choose between the two on the night Jesus was betrayed, he compromised.
>
> Thomas had to have everything proven to him. This is the logical mind of [analysers]. They want documentation. The logical approach may help an [analyser] go over the

> edge to accept Christ, but, of course you cannot live on logic alone.

Burgess cautions about distorting the message by tailoring it too tightly to the personality and the person before us. 'We can try to base people's Christianity in terms of social satisfaction,' he says, 'but that is not the true basis of Christianity. You can't temper true Christianity and dilute the real meaning of Christ.' For example, Burgess says that we shouldn't tell entertainers to become a Christian because they will have fun and make lots of new friends. If their decision is based on that, it is selfish and unbiblical. Using personality information to better relate the message of Christ is fine, but we cannot distort the message so that it no longer represents true Christianity.

Above all, this personality-profile specialist emphasises the importance of leaving room for the Spirit to work.

> The Holy Spirit is very instructive with how to witness, with what to say and reveal, and with dealing with the weaknesses of each personality style. If we're trying to witness in our own style alone, without the help of the Holy Spirit, all our worst traits will come into play. What it really comes down to is letting the Holy Spirit be a part of the witness and not trying to do it on our own. Jesus commissioned us to spread the Good News, but the burden of proof rests with the Holy Spirit.

The common denominator among Christians everywhere is that *everyone*, regardless of personality, has the same task. We cannot sidestep our responsibility to show Christ's love within us and tell others about him. Jesus asked, 'Who then is the faithful and wise servant, whom the master has put in charge of the servants in his household to give them their food at the proper time? It will be good for that servant whose master finds him doing so when he returns' (Matt. 24:45–46).

Analyser Curt, a customer-service speaker, said, 'We're letting the minority dictate the policies for the majority on issues like religious assemblies in schools. It is similar to when someone writes a bad cheque. All of a sudden, the store imposes rules for everyone else. It is time for the majority – Christians – to speak out.

'If we remain silent about what we believe,' Curt added, 'which is the easy way, nothing changes. By continuing to be silent, we choose to be part of the problem.' And, I might add, we are also disobeying God.

In *Who You Are When No One's Looking*, Bill Hybels writes, 'If it takes courage to *become* a Christian, it takes even more courage to *be* a Christian.' My prayer is that you will find some of that courage in the following chapters as fellow Christians share their stories about how they witness in a way that is right for them.

Getting Started

1. Remind yourself of Christ's command that you tell others about him. Read Matthew 10:27; 16:24–26; 28:19–20; Mark 13:10; 16:15–16; Luke 12:8–9; Romans 10:14–15.
2. Remind yourself that God gives many different spiritual gifts. Read 1 Corinthians 12:1–20.
3. List the special gifts God has given you to use in Christ's service.
4. List specific ways you can use these gifts to fulfil Christ's command to tell others about him.

12

From One Director to Another

Every personality comes with a certain set of assumptions. The secular world expects the director to be outgoing, aggressive and successful, while the Christian sector assumes this outspoken powerhouse will prove to be the proverbial pillar of strength when witnessing. Of course, the biggest flaw with any assumption is making it in the first place! Let me explain away the 'pillar of witnessing strength' myth with the rest of my story.

The concept for this book originated from a lecture I gave at the Evangelical Association of New England (EANE) annual conference in Boston in 1992. The seminar and original manuscript title was 'Witnessing for Wimps' and consisted of a first-person account of an 'ordinary Christian' and her struggle to follow the Great Commission. That 'ordinary Christian' was me.

Cowardly Beginnings

You'll easily see why a director could be a witnessing wimp when you consider that we don't like being out of control or looking stupid. Personally speaking, I didn't like the image of the Bible-thumping, holy-roller, stand-on-the-street-corner, born-again Christian. It was unprofessional and embarrassing. If that was witnessing, I didn't want any part of it.

Stephen Brown writes about this in *No More Mr Nice Guy*. He says a Christian can be bold as long as that boldness is characterised by love. Without love, the whole point of boldness is lost. 'Anybody can be bold,' he says, 'but to be lovingly bold is no small thing. Love remembers the other person. Love looks out for the interest of others. Love is sometimes harsh, strong, and even angry, but it is never destructive. Christian boldness is a boldness that never forgets the other person.'

Along the same line, an analyser pastor explains, 'Christ does not abuse us, belittle us or put us down. We cannot put other people down or deny their beliefs. We are not called to stand on the street corner and ask, "Are you saved?" This is a scary and bizarre approach. You can do a lot of damage and turn a lot of people off religion for ever.'

Two experiences on plane trips helped me work out that the trick is to stay away from what turns people off and to share my faith in a way that is comfortable for me.

The first incident happened when I took my son to visit his grandparents one August. We were on a sold-out flight and had to make a quick change of planes at the other end. Being a typical mother, I looked at the tight itinerary and insisted that Jason use the facilities on the plane since he wouldn't have much time while we were on the ground. I carefully edged out of my aisle seat, taking care not to disturb the gentleman in front of me, who had his seat reclined. As I was standing in the aisle letting my son out of his seat, this man, whom I had never spoken to before in my life, turned to me and said, 'Has your pastor preached the Revelation?'

Pardon? What did this total stranger just say to me?

What exactly did this well-meaning person seek to accomplish? Did he expect to get into a lengthy discussion (or debate) about the end of the world? Was he using fear of death to try to jolt me into inviting Christ into my life? Did he expect me to say, 'Yes! Praise the Lord!'?

Whatever remote good he thought he was doing was entirely lost because of his over-abrupt and offensive manner. Before I took my seat, I turned to him and quietly said, 'That is an interesting introductory comment coming from a total stranger.' Here was one more confirmation that witnessing was definitely not for me.

A few weeks later I was flying back from a week-long photography workshop. Classes were held from 8 a.m. until 11 p.m., and I had spent no time reading my Bible the entire week. I decided to catch up on the plane home.

During the taxi and take-off I was holding my Bible on my lap. It occurred to me my neighbour might think I was 'clutching' my Bible because I was nervous about the flight. Not wanting my supposed nervousness to cause him any undue anxiety, I explained my plan to catch up on my reading.

We spent the next three hours chatting amiably about the various joys and challenges we each faced with our Christian walk. It turned out we had each moved house within the past year and had yet to make an effort to find and join a local Bible-believing church. By the time the plane touched down, we each agreed our next step was to find a new church.

The second plane 'witnessing' experience was one of the nicest, most unpretentious experiences I had ever had talking about Christ with a total stranger. As a direct result of that conversation, we both promptly and actively rejoined churches. Also, for the first time ever, I realised there was a way to share faith without being unprofessional or embarrassing.

Some people might consider the first experience up-front witnessing and the second experience fellowship with another believer. I consider the first *insanity* and the second *serendipity*. My casual opening *was* a possible lead into witnessing; it required taking a deep breath and launching a conversation with a stranger. It just happened that my neighbour was a Christian, not an unbeliever.

Don't Smother the Spirit

After the second experience I wanted to find ways to share my faith, and I found my answer in 1 Thessalonians 5:19: 'Do not put out the Spirit's fire.' I stopped expecting God to make a plane carry a banner across the sky telling me when and where and what and how, and I began listening to the quiet tap, tap, tapping in my soul. Instead of waiting for a big vision, I adopted the policy that I wrote about earlier – just not ducking from opportunities that popped up.

My first experience with EANE was actually the 1991 Congress. I set my alarm clock for 5 a.m. and drove for two hours amid rush-hour traffic to look at the resources in the 'trade show'. (My home town offers almost nothing by way of Christian books, tapes and supplies.) I had no idea the event was so huge! More than six thousand Christians attended that year, and scores of others were turned away because the building was at maximum capacity.

As I sat in on seminars, I was struck by the fact that nearly all of the lecturers were 'professional Christians'. The director in me thought automatically of volunteering, but the reigning wimp quickly squashed that idea. After all, I wasn't a pastor, church leader or evangelist. I was just a plain, common or garden Christian.

Then came the tap, tap, tapping on my heart.

After six months of silently shouting no to the Holy Spirit's steady knocking, I wrote to EANE, offering to do a workshop for wimps the following year. Not expecting (or really wanting) EANE to respond, I quickly scribbled a barely legible note outlining my idea and dropped it in the post.

The next day EANE phoned to accept my suggestion – my proposal had arrived the very day the committee was making final selections for the speaking roster.

Some people don't have the courage to go out of their way looking for opportunities as I did, nor do they always need to. Carol, a director, says God seems to put her in situations where she cannot help but share her faith. She cites a recent trip with her husband to Denmark, where their son was an exchange student.

'We were seated around the dinner table at the home where our son was staying and comparing notes about different issues adults care about. I had commented that I had read Denmark has the highest tax rate in the world, so our hosts were explaining the various things the taxes pay for. They said there is an automatic 1 per cent tax that goes directly to the Church. The very outspoken [director] hostess explained they do have the option to delete that particular tax, and she said she took the option since she does not believe in the Church or in God.

'I knew there was no way I could keep my mouth shut on that one,' says Carol. 'So I took a deep breath and launched in while my peacekeeper husband gently pressed his foot on top of mine under the table to remind me we were guests in their home.

'Since I was dealing with someone as outspoken as myself,

I knew I had to be direct and get right to the point. I asked her specific questions about what she believed. I asked her why. I asked her why she didn't believe in God and in Jesus Christ. She had a pretty wishy-washy faith in nature, and she couldn't offer any concrete answers that would convince me to listen to and respect her faith. As recently as a year ago, I never would have said anything to this woman, particularly while our family were guests in her home, but I've come to the conclusion that if I am not going to knock on doors or travel to remote corners of Africa, I need and want to share my faith where God puts me. During that year I had spent time reading and thinking about my faith. Because I had taken the initiative to prepare my mind, I felt quite competent and confident to share what I believe and why.

'The material I gave her was right out of Paul Little's *Know Why You Believe* and his *Know What You Believe.* I talked about how the apostles who ran in fear the night Jesus was arrested spoke out forty days later at Pentecost in the very city where they had feared for their lives. I also pointed out that each disciple ultimately died a martyr's death. I talked about the empty tomb and the many people who saw Jesus after the resurrection and before the ascension.

'I pointed out that the first Christians were Jewish, grounded in the tradition of worshipping on Saturday, and yet gathered on Sunday to worship Jesus and celebrate the resurrection. I said that on top of all this historical information, I continue to see a huge change in my own life from who I was before I accepted Jesus Christ to who I am now.'

Carol admits, 'I don't think the mother heard a word I said, but I know her teenage son was impressed that I knew what I believed in and why and that I didn't leave my brains at the church door.'

Michelle, another director, says she is not always clear whether she is acting impulsively à la director or if God is truly speaking. For example, she decided to tackle the issue of prayer within her profession. As a new appointee to her professional organisation's board of directors, she says it seemed odd to offer grace at the public gala awards reception at the annual conference and not offer grace before the monthly dinner meetings where the planning was actually being done for the conference. The inconsistency made her feel like a hypocrite. 'I kept quiet at the first meeting,' says Michelle, 'because I figured I was just thinking and acting impulsively.

'But during the entire two-hour drive to the next meeting, the issue weighed heavy on my heart, and I knew the Holy Spirit was calling for me to speak out. I also knew I didn't want to open up a can of worms! Yet the Holy Spirit kept knocking at my heart, so I turned off the car stereo and opened my mind and my heart to God. Then, at the meeting, with my heart pounding and my hands shaking, I expressed my concern over the prayer inconsistency to the twenty-five members on the board of directors. A few of my peers heckled me, but others nodded in agreement. I offered grace.

'They don't always stop to offer grace, and they sometimes direct a sarcastic comment my way. But I feel like I remained true to my faith and true to God's call to speak out.' Michelle adds, 'About a year later our regional trade journal carried a lengthy editorial about how offensive prayers are when "inconsiderate" Christians end their awards reception grace by saying, "in the name of Jesus Christ, Amen". Once again I felt called to speak out, so I drafted a letter to the president of the organisation.

'Instead of taking issue with the topic of prayer, I said the ongoing lengthy editorials had become a personal soapbox for the editor, they wasted precious space in an already too small publication, and the views misrepresented the membership to anyone who might chance across the newsletter. I let the reply sit on my desk a few days. After my cooling-off time had elapsed and I reread the letter, I knew the Holy Spirit was leading me to respond.

'By speaking out,' concludes Michelle, 'I was able to prevent the issue of prayer from being dragged through the mud in a heavily slanted publication. I also voiced the opinion of the silent majority, Christians, who did and do want prayer as a part of their professional lives.'

Stop, Drop, Roll

To determine whether an idea comes from God or from herself, Michelle uses the same advice firefighters offer to someone whose clothing has caught fire: Stop. Drop. Roll. Stop what you are doing *before* you make a decision. Drop on your knees. Roll the issue over to God. You may be thinking you don't always have time to pray, but in the words of Oswald Chambers, 'What can be more important than prayer?' If the issue has moral importance and stays with you during and after your prayer, you can feel certain it comes from God.

'The funny thing about all of this,' says Michelle, 'is that I have never been very good at prayer, particularly public prayer. I am having to *learn* how to pray because now I am consistently asked to offer the grace at all kinds of professional gatherings. Whoever asks me is always so thankful and so relieved that I am willing to take on this awkward task. Isn't it sad that anyone should think of prayer as being a "task" or as being "awkward"?'

When I apply the stop, drop and roll concept to my own

life, I slow down just enough to listen to God. That seems to help reduce my automatic-volunteer mode. And I no longer feel guilty about not doing the things I am not good at. I'm an organiser and a motivator, but I'm not the person to serve on the altar guild or the kitchen committee. I also used to sink down in the pew when the call came for Sunday-school teachers or holiday-Bible-club leaders. Tedious details bore me to tears, and the group chaos of small children makes me unbelievably tense. I'm happy to do the jobs that scare off the peacekeepers and analysers, because I do not want to have anything to do with the jobs that are suited for them!

When Duty Calls

Since success often launches directors into the limelight at early ages, they have lots of opportunities to witness outside church. That doesn't mean they don't have excuses. When God called Jeremiah to be a prophet, he protested that he wasn't the right person for the job because he was just a youth. God replied, 'Do not say, "I am only a child." You must go to everyone I send you to and say whatever I command you. Do not be afraid of them, for I am with you and will rescue you' (Jer. 1:7–8). God knew Jeremiah better than Jeremiah knew himself.

Insurance sales professional Charles puts it this way: 'A witness is someone who has been converted by the Holy Spirit. The secret is never to *try* to witness. As your new nature offsets the old, the Holy Spirit witnesses through you all the time.

'I have done two-hour business meetings where I didn't once mention anything religious, and someone will come up afterwards and comment on my being a Christian merely because of my words and actions.'

When it comes to witnessing at work, Charles suggests simply making yourself available to God and to those who need to hear the Word of God. Charles says, 'I also realised it would be important for me to be the best I could be in my company. I never set out to make money *per se*, but I knew before any of my peers would listen to what I had to say about Christ, they would first have to respect me on a business level. For me the secret is to work harder, give more and be better.'

In *My Utmost for His Highest* Oswald Chambers writes about the great need for the Christian worker to be ready to face Jesus Christ everywhere. He must have had the director in mind when he wrote, 'The battle is not against sin or difficulties or circumstances, but against being so absorbed in work that we are not ready to face Jesus at every turn. Expect to find Jesus at every turn in the child-like wonder he wants us to have.'

Norman Vincent Peale said he was often asked why he included Christ in a business or motivation programme. His reason was simple: 'I do not believe real self improvement is possible apart from God working in our lives.'

I have used all this advice for the foundation of my business practices, and I always use the honesty issue as an opportunity to talk a little about my faith in front of four or five hundred professional photographers during my lectures. I begin by relating to what my audience can visualise: black-and-white photography.

Most black-and-white photography has a gradation of tones from zero to ten (as in Ansel Adams's zone system). The majority of the image is more grey than it is black or white. On a lithograph all the grey tones are deliberately removed so the image is entirely black and white. Most photographers do not offer this product because it involves more work.

With the picture of these two similar yet strikingly different products in mind, I challenge the members of the audience to operate their businesses like the lithograph photograph. No grey space! I may say something like 'Everything I ever needed to know about business I learned in Sunday school. My faith calls me to be honest and forthright and to stay out of the grey.'

Perhaps directors' greatest witness is to break out of the mould of their secular counterparts, rely on the gifts of the Spirit to overcome their faults and stay clearly out of the grey. 'Whatever is true, whatever is noble, whatever is right, whatever is pure, whatever is lovely, whatever is admirable – if anything is excellent or praiseworthy – think about such things' (Phil. 4:8).

13

What Entertainers Have to Say

Since entertainers have such easygoing natures, love for people and ease with public speaking, all the other personalities assume they also come with built-in desires and abilities for witnessing. However, the witnessing statistics I cited earlier indicate that entertainers themselves don't necessarily agree with this assumption! As with all personalities, deep-rooted fears within entertainers work against their desire to share their faith. When you consider that the entertainer's big fear in life is social disapproval, the last thing this person wants is to appear a 'Converter Christian'.

To combat this fear of losing face, entertainers should impress on themselves the ultimate end of their family members, friends and business colleagues. Risking separation from them in this life by witnessing to them may prevent an eternal separation from them. And who else will tell them about Jesus – the way, the truth and the life? Probably no one.

Think about it. What are the odds of your mother or sister or friend at the office really hearing and listening to the words of Jesus? Many things might lead your unsaved friends to Christ – osmosis, television or radio, doorstep evangelists, newspaper or magazine articles, revivals, heavenly visions,

Bible study, tracts or religious books, contemporary Christian music, Sunday-school teachers, youth-group ministries, testimony of strangers, visits of a minister – but nothing has the impact of the witness of family members or friends.

'Anyone who calls upon the name of the Lord will be saved. But how shall they ask him to save them unless they believe in him? And how can they believe in him if they have never heard about him? And how can they hear about him unless someone tells them?' (Romans 10:13–14 LB).

Finding the Right Time and Place

Sometimes you have to plan an opportunity in order to witness. Pastor John Maxwell suggests role-playing with non-Christian friends and family. You might say, 'We're doing this class at our church on how to share your beliefs and faith. Do you mind if I practise on you? It would help me a lot if you would let me know when I explain something well and when I am not very clear. This way I can get better.'

Maxwell goes on to say, 'Before you've had time to agonise over getting it "right", you have spent fifteen or twenty minutes sharing your faith and explaining about the saving grace of Jesus. Your friend has been listening because he or she wants to help you as a friend.'

For the apostle Peter, any time was a good time to witness. Just moments after being released from jail and warned not to preach any more, Peter was back on the street corner loudly proclaiming the gospel. When Peter was promptly arrested again, the high priest demanded to know why he insisted on flouting the authorities. Peter replied, 'We must obey God rather than men!' (Acts 5:29). Of course Peter didn't go through an easy process to become so self-assured.

Recall that on the night of Christ's arrest this same man quailed before three citizens who identified him as Christ's follower. He denied it: 'I don't know the man!' (Matt. 26:74).

While Peter's denial was extreme, entertainers can also feel the need to compromise when the Spirit tells us the time is right to witness. Pastor Stephen Brown shared his story at a gathering of five thousand Christians. He explained that business leaders frequently asked him to speak after dinner meetings. He would tell a few jokes and talk about the good things of God so everyone went away feeling happy. Then Stephen came to know the Lord on a very personal basis, and his conviction to share this relationship much outweighed his desire to tell a few jokes and stories.

At the next meeting, as he sat at the top table, his neighbours played 'Shock the Reverend', and his confidence waned. He began to think that he might be better off reverting to his previous talk. As he considered this, a friend who had also recently made a deep commitment to Christ walked over to him and said, 'Don't back down one bit. I am praying for you!' Stephen went on to deliver the message God had called him to present.

If a long-time personal associate of Jesus and a twentieth-century pulpit preacher can worry about what people will say, no wonder 'ordinary' entertainer Christians stammer and stumble! If you are looking for the perfect time and place to share the best possible message before you begin witnessing, you might be seeking an ideal that doesn't exist.

Karen, a nurse who often gives professional workshops for her peers, regularly shares her enthusiasm for Christ with her secular audiences. Although she may witness in front of one hundred nurses several times a month, she says it *never* seems the right time or the right place.

'After every lecture I feel so vulnerable. Even when I get a wonderful reception, I am literally sick for the whole of the next day. Although I am not always comfortable witnessing, I have always felt obligated to share Christ. That is probably because I am so grateful,' she explained. 'I know the difference Christ has made in my life.'

Karen suggests keeping the witness upbeat. 'I always keep an attitude of gratitude. That is also why I keep sharing my faith. I am so thankful. I don't condemn. I just share. I want people to see that the love of Christ is great and that I want them to have it too.

'Witnessing should be very believable. It should be a natural extension of yourself. You don't have to have a great memory or give a great speech. I can't seem to remember Scripture. I'm not good at that. Just come from the perspective of one human being sharing with another. Tell them what is in your heart. I say, "He loves me. He loves you. That is the secret." It's not very eloquent, but it's real.'

Karen also tries to drop enough bits and pieces into daily conversations at work to let her patients know she is a Christian. 'I usually say something in the form of a third-party story. For example, I like to talk about the stories I tell my Sunday-school class. Once, when I was explaining to the children how much Jesus loves them, I related it to what kids love – dogs. I talked about how a dog may do something wrong and then get spanked by its master. I told the children that, of course, the master still loves the dog. A kid can understand this story, and so can my patients.

'Somehow, during the next week at work, I'll tie this story into what I might be talking about while I'm working with a patient. The patient gets my message from the story in a simple and unobtrusive way without breaking up the health-care business at hand.

'I always assume the patient is in this with me. My

conversation about how great God's love is always includes them. If they don't know Christ already, they cannot object to my including them. Also,' she added, 'they might begin to wonder how they can get this love and joy too.'

A Bolder Approach

Mark, a small-business owner, said, 'Go out and make loads of mistakes! It seems you either like witnessing or you don't. It either comes easily or it doesn't. There seems to be this huge gap. We can close that gap by just getting out there.

'Witnessing, to me, means sharing my faith in Christ and the reality and the simplicity of the example of Christ. I'm an opportunity seizer. I walk through the day with my eyes open. Then I seize and take hold. I am as bold as I think I can be with each opportunity. Sometimes I stop myself short. It is more than common sense. It's listening to what God is telling my heart. If the time hasn't come, I back off.'

Calling his witnessing style very free and spontaneous, Mark said his number one message is a personal relationship with the Lord. 'I am not a fire-and-brimstone or letter-of-the-law witness. I want to explain that God is not a white collar or a padded pew. He is someone who wants to have a personal relationship with you.'

To get his message across, he will often simply tell the story of how he and his wife made a definite commitment to Christ in 1976. 'People can argue with Scripture or rules,' says Mark, 'but they cannot dispute my testimony.'

Using the Entertainer's Flair

Betty calls herself an analyser who masquerades as an entertainer. (She was the sceptical teenager who told the pastor she really didn't believe in the message of Jesus Christ.) While Betty can be spontaneous, she says her Christianity puts this trait into play in areas where she wouldn't venture if she weren't a Christian.

'I was in the baker's when a woman was buying an enormous order. It was summer, and the queue stretched out of the door. Though I was next in line after her, I tapped her on the shoulder and offered to help carry her purchases out to the car. It might seem like a simple thing, but without Jesus Christ in my life, I doubt I would have offered to give up my place in the queue and help out a total stranger.

'Another time I was in the supermarket and a toddler who was tired of grocery shopping with her mother was yelling her head off. I always carry a kazoo in my pocket, so I got it out and started playing "You Are My Sunshine" in front of everyone. I'm sure that was motivated by the Christian in me.'

The Relationship Approach

Karen, an entertainer housewife and mother of two small children, said, 'I have no trouble talking to anyone about anything except my faith. When it comes to witnessing, I have always shared with the people I already know. I usually share a specific element of my faith that helps them to deal with some problem in their life.' When talking doesn't work, she writes letters.

One friend's husband frequently took the Lord's name in vain. It particularly bothered the wife because their two-year-old son was beginning to pick up the bad habit. 'I knew she must have a sense of love for the Lord,' Karen comments, 'or she wouldn't care about the swearing. So I invited her to my place. We went over some things in the Bible that related to her problem. Later, I couldn't get the idea of writing her a letter out of my head. I stopped everything – no easy task with two small children – and wrote to her. I talked about the concerns she had been sharing about her husband, and I wrote down all the Bible verses I could find that related.'

Letter writing helped another time when Karen wrote to a family friend's wife, who was suffering from severe morning sickness. 'Since this woman doesn't really let people get close to her, I knew it wasn't going to be very easy to reach her. I could relate to her problem because I had also had bad morning sickness, so I wrote her a letter.' Karen adds, 'When I witness, I usually share from my own life. That opens a door to share about the gospel, about the forgiveness of sins, about love and about the promise of eternal life.'

David, a photographer, also puts his faith in writing, the final step in his three-part witnessing. This entertainer regularly opens his portrait studio to week-long classes to teach his photography skills, and I saw his witnessing in action when I was his student a few years back.

Throughout the week David makes a point of offering verbal testimony by telling brief stories here and there that relate directly, or indirectly, to the photography topics at hand. He also shows that he lives his faith through his impeccable business practices. He ties the stories and the lifestyle examples together with a two-page letter to each student at the completion of the course. He opens the letter by offering his personal testimony. Then he points out that the reader is extremely valuable in the eyes of the Lord:

> He would die for you, and you alone. All you have to do is receive this love, this forgiveness, and this guarantee of eternal salvation by accepting Jesus Christ as Lord and Saviour, and asking for forgiveness of your sins . . . He will forgive you and cleanse you and actually 'forget' your

> transgressions. It is an amazing love. Don't live your life without it. It is too great a joy to miss.

The letter ends with an invitation to contact David, and he offers several of his favourite verses. He also includes a poem he wrote, 'Truly Wealthy', which focuses on his gratitude to God.

David says he includes the letter with the class handouts at the end of the week for several reasons. He readily admits he is a witnessing wimp and just plain worried about what people will think of him. On the practical side, he says he doesn't want to scare people away or turn them off by being too outspoken or pushy. He sets the mood with his stories, sets the example with his lifestyle and business practices, and then offers the letter to touch the heart of anyone who is interested in finding out more about why he is so content, so peaceful and so full of joy. He expects that students will read the letter out of curiosity, if nothing else!

What Entertainers Say About Failing

Entertainer Jim, a Christian for twenty years who has college-age kids, said he used to feel bad that he had never actually led someone to Christ. He said no matter how often he witnessed, no one – friend or stranger – felt moved to invite the Lord into his or her heart. It hurt his ego that he wasn't actually 'saving' anyone. Jim said the turning point for him came when someone pointed out the parable of the sowers and the reapers. He realised he had his task to do while other Christians had theirs.

> Do you not say, 'Four months more and then the harvest'? I tell you, open your eyes and look at the fields! They are

> ripe for harvest. Even now the reaper draws his wages, even now he harvests the crop for eternal life, so that the sower and the reaper may be glad together. Thus the saying 'One sows and another reaps' is true. I sent you to reap what you have not worked for. Others have done the hard work, and you have reaped the benefits of their labour. (John 4:35–38).

Since Jim does the sowing part of witnessing, he has to deal with the inevitable stings when the seeds fall on rocky soil. 'Every now and then you get flattened,' Jim muses. 'During the first two or three years after I became a Christian I remember reaching out to hold a woman's hand and asking her if she wanted to pray. She snapped her hand back and said, "Absolutely not!"

'It surprises me when people respond that way, because who *wouldn't* want the love of Jesus Christ? For some reason, other than being surprised, it doesn't really bother me when this happens. I am generally super-sensitive, so you would think this would crush me. Instead of thinking about it as failure, I focus on my confidence in Jesus Christ.'

Paul, an entertainer who also accepted the Lord when he was an adult, said, 'I've been roasted! I visited a lawyer who has an office near mine. He's an alcoholic and was in hospital. Although I usually see my role as concentrating on the good stuff, I felt a deep conviction to show this man the other side. Instead of selling the good parts, I put it to him bluntly and pointed out the obvious sin in his life.

'He laughed at me. Not just then, but for ever after whenever he would see me at work. The lesson I learned from this is that *you* don't have to *save* anyone. The Holy Spirit does the convicting. You just have to open your mouth and share the love that is Jesus Christ.'

14

The Powerful Witness of the Peacekeeper

At the Last Supper Jesus spoke to his disciples: 'A new command I give you: Love one another. As I have loved you, so you must love one another. By this all men will know that you are my disciples, if you love one another' (John 13:34–35). Peacekeepers, above all other personalities, have taken these words to heart. However, most of them don't realise that they have done so.

Almost all the peacekeepers I interviewed honestly believed they had little to say about witnessing because they weren't good at it. These peacekeepers are members of my church or personal acquaintances whom I have long admired and respected as being good witnesses. Once again, a false assumption gets in the way.

Peacekeepers assume the only real witness is an outspoken crusader for Christ. The assumption follows that since they cannot be outspoken, they cannot truly witness. The irony is that the witness that most touches the hearts of many directors and entertainers is the life and words and deeds of gentle peacekeepers.

Remember, for example, the story of the director student who had razor blades ready to slice her wrists. She didn't die that day because of the flashbacks to words from her peacekeeper Sunday-school teachers.

Contemporary Christian rock musician Ray Boltz glorifies these unsung heroes with his song 'Thank You'. He thanks the person who, because the pictures made him cry, gave the little money he had to a missionary. He sings about an eight year old who bowed his head in Sunday school and invited Jesus into his heart, and he sings about all the people who were touched by small generosities, little things that someone said and did on behalf of the Lord.

Just as in the song, people have lined up to tell me about a particular peacekeeper's wonderful witness. Analyser Mark said his desire to become a minister dates back to when he was a three year old attending a Sunday-school class in the church basement. 'The teacher taught us to sing, "The B-I-B-L-E, yes that's the book for me." I went home and announced to my parents that I was going to be a minister when I grew up.' Mark adds, 'The most enormous witnesses I have ever known are ones who live out their witness. They are so Christlike in what they say and do that I want to be like them.'

Marcelle, the octogenarian director at our church, agreed: 'Many times I did not realise how powerful someone's quiet witness was until many years later. Only now, looking back through the years, do I realise how many peacekeeper Christians have helped to keep my faith strong.'

My story also includes many examples of the powerful witness of a gentle peacekeeper. I didn't realise just how many until last autumn, when I volunteered to give the sermon. After mulling over possible topics, I decided to encourage the congregation to witness by sharing the ways different people have witnessed to me. After I sat down and compiled my stories, I was amazed at how many included the quiet witness of peacekeepers.

My story began with the Sunday-school and holiday-Bible-club teachers at Trinity, my childhood church. The organist and youth-group leader, Clem, whom I mentioned earlier, came next. Primarily because of her influence, I had offered to take over our own church youth group.

During my time attending Trinity, my parents got divorced, and I faced the possibility of spending my last year at school as a 'foreigner' in a small town twenty miles away. To enable me to stay on at 'my' school, Harold and Doris offered to give me room and board. No rules. No stipulations. No checking up on me – even when I gave them plenty of reason to! This gentle retired couple opened their home and their hearts to a teenager they barely knew.

The next peacekeeper influence came during my early married years, when Mike was stationed at Coast Guard Air Station Cape Cod and I was stationed in Newport, sixty-two miles away. We lived at the air force base on Cape Cod, and because of the commuting we didn't have much time to get to know anyone. That was when we first encountered the hospitality of John and Leanne. They invited us to share Thanksgiving dinner with their family because they knew we were three thousand miles from home. But we were new at their church and felt too silly to accept the invitation of virtual strangers.

It became an annual invitation, although we continually declined. Finally, after ten years we accepted. It was the nicest Thanksgiving we have ever had (and yes, Leanne asked again the next year!). Their witness has been more than just turkey dinners. Through the years we have watched, admired, envied and finally imitated the love they have for each other, for their children and for the Lord.

Although the worst of the wobble has gone out of my walk with the Lord, peacekeepers continue to be my stable, loving, helpful supporters. Pam is a perfect example. This peacekeeper is the mother of two of my youth-group kids, and she is *always* there. She supports her children, the youth group, and me and my hare-brained ideas. Cleaning up after a spaghetti supper, hanging decorations for a church dance, chaperoning a carload of kids on a Christmas shopping expedition to a shopping centre miles away, or traipsing off to camp in the middle of sixty-five thousand people at a Christian music festival – Pam is always there.

The Bible offers similar examples of the steady witness of people like Pam. When Tabitha, who sewed for the needy at Joppa, suddenly died, the believers there mourned. Hearing that Peter was nearby, they urged him to come. Peter prayed and brought her back to life. Many people heard of the miracle of Tabitha and believed in the Lord. But to the poor she had helped, Tabitha's witness was her needle.

Oswald Chambers writes about the service of the peacekeeper in *My Utmost for His Highest*.

> Service is the natural part of my life. God gets me into a relationship with Himself whereby I understand His call, then I do things out of sheer love for Him on my own account. To serve God is the deliberate love-gift of a nature that has heard the call of God . . . The Son of God reveals Himself in me, and I serve Him in the ordinary ways of life out of devotion to Him.

Witnessing, for the peacekeeper, begins with accepting *service* as a legitimate part of sharing the gospel. Just as the apostle Peter struggled to overcome fear of social disapproval, peacekeepers have struggled to accept service as being a worthy witness. For example, a brother once complained to St Francis of Assisi about the bishop's not allowing brothers to preach to people. St Francis replied that brothers 'convert them, as the rule ordains, more by our example than by our words'.

Grace and Forgiveness

The spiritual gifts of grace and forgiveness are almost second nature for the peacekeeper. Consider this story from author and speaker Philip Yancey. A girl from the country came to the city to get away from squabbling with her father. The pretty young woman was wined and dined and enticed into becoming a prostitute. She also became hooked on drugs. In two years her beauty was gone and her money was gone. In January she was sleeping over a heating grate in a seedy part of town.

Just like the prodigal son in Jesus's parable, she realised that the cocker spaniels at home had life easier than she did. She sent a postcard to her father, telling him that he did not have to take her back into the family. She said she was catching a bus home, and if she saw a yellow ribbon tied to the banister on the front porch, she would know her father wanted her. If not, she wouldn't bother to get off the bus.

She found a few more clients and scraped together the money for the ticket. When the bus rounded the corner of her sleepy home town, she saw a yellow ribbon tied around every tree lining the street. As she stepped off the bus with her apology on her lips, her father said, 'Hush, child. We have a celebration party to go to.' No abrasive condemnation from a director. No dripping sarcasm from an entertainer. No cutting criticism from an analyser. Just the genuine acceptance of a loving peacekeeper.

Some might say she was accepted home by a loving *father* not a loving *peacekeeper*. Maybe. I would like to think I would accept my own son home so readily, but I know the reality is that my 'director' would inevitably get in the way. I am a loving mother, but a loving mother who gets tripped up all the time in my readiness to direct. Only as I allow the Holy Spirit to work in my life will that abrasive condemnation dissolve so I can fling my arms wide with a genuine peacekeeper welcome-home embrace.

Where would the world be without the open arms and the nurturing words of the peacekeeper?

When Peacekeepers Are Ready to Talk

Lenin taught that you change people by changing society, but Jesus teaches that you change society by changing people. By creating a deep moral change in the hearts of individuals through the gospel of Jesus Christ, you will ultimately change people, who will then change the world.

Peacekeepers say a good way to begin being more verbal about witnessing is to write a short paragraph of your own story. Jot down a little bit about your life before you knew Christ, how or why you were spiritually reborn, and what your life is like now. If you accepted Christ when you were quite young, you could write down the difference your faith has made compared to your secular friends.

Charles E. Jones, author of *Life Is Tremendous*, says just mentioning the name Jesus Christ reverently, and not in vain, is a strong witness. When writing down and later sharing your testimony, he suggests talking about *the* Church, not *my* church. 'You don't argue who has the best mother, so why argue about who has the best church?' Jones points out. 'The real church is the one you are born into in your heart. Also, you don't have to give a good performance. Just get across your motive for sharing and let God do the rest.'

For many peacekeepers, just the act of writing their innermost feelings of what Christ and Christianity mean to them helps get them started. The next step is to share this paragraph with a Christian friend. (You're welcome to knock on your neighbour's door and recite the paragraph, but the point is this exercise is to encourage you and not scare you off!)

Writing a paragraph and then sharing it with a friend is so simple it almost seems silly. Yet when a speaker at a Christian conference I attended unexpectedly asked us to pair off and do just this, it was the first time I had ever actually given a spoken testimony. Just about everyone in the room said the same thing. Since then I've done the same impromptu sharing exchange in all my lectures. Every time we safely share our story with a fellow Christian, our faith becomes that much more real, and our witnessing becomes that much easier.

Easing into It

Lifestyle or friendship evangelism begins by talking to people who touch your life in some way. You don't look to the world at large, but to your mate at work or your friend at school. You will be a lot more comfortable if you ease your faith into the conversation as early as possible. The longer you wait, the more difficult it will become to bring up the subject.

You don't need to have 'I am a Christian' tattooed on your forehead to make your point. An offhand comment here and there will do the job. For example, if I am talking to someone about weekend plans, I may mention that Mike gets into the office early on Saturday since he comes directly from the men's breakfast at our church, or I might talk about what activity I'm planning for the Sunday evening youth fellowship meeting. Once the ice has been broken and people know we are 'religious', it is much easier to bring up Christianity later on.

Stephanie, a secondary-school student, said most of her friends know she is a Christian. 'My faith and my church are so much a part of my life that it is easy to talk about them to my friends. Whenever we drive past my church, I always point it out to my friends. I'm really proud of our church, and I want my friends to know I go there. I also regularly talk about the things we do at church and with the youth group so my friends know about that part of my life.'

Stephanie's way of witnessing at school is to make a point of being extra nice to the less popular kids. 'There are always a couple of kids that no one seems to like. The church has taught me to think of all people the same, so I will make an extra effort to draw those kids in and give them a chance.'

Stephanie has gradually had more confidence to talk about her faith more specifically with these friends who know she is a Christian. A friend who worships nature challenged her faith in God and Jesus Christ by saying there was no proof. Stephanie's youth group had been studying why they believe and what they believe, so she felt comfortable answering her sceptical friend. She said it was an easy way to witness because the friend already knew she was a Christian and he actually initiated the conversation. These conversations ultimately enabled her friend to feel comfortable enough with 'religion' to attend a Christian rock youth rally with her.

Joan, who runs a hospital clinic, uses her peacekeeper

nature with the ill. 'In working with so many sick people,' she says, 'I have come to realise that a lot of people really do have faith, but it is buried deep inside. With all of their current physical ills, it can be even harder for them to rediscover their faith. I try to make them as comfortable as possible to help relieve their physical problems. Then they can find the faith they've buried. I don't push religion so much as I push faith.'

Pam, a housewife and mother of two, says, 'The one thing I do that is very important to me is teach my children about being a Christian. I want to prepare them so when they come to the struggles in their own lives they will have a strong foundation to stand on.

'My own faith was badly shaken when my father died. It took a while to gradually build my faith back up. I weave my faith into little actions and comments in everyday life so faith will be alive for my children.' Pam adds that she has always envied the outspoken organiser skills of the director. In true peacekeeper style she says, 'All I can be is helpful, and that just doesn't seem enough.'

A Quiet Witness Speaks Out

As I mentioned earlier, I have long admired Leanne. Her gentle manner, kind words, gracious hospitality and steady devotion have been an ongoing inspiration to me. With this project in mind, I asked her to explain how her view of witnessing has evolved through the years.

'My Catholic upbringing taught me it was almost like scoring points with God to share Christ with others. When I became a born-again Christian, the message changed. The sermons made me feel that people are out there drowning and I was ignoring them. All of a sudden, I felt personally responsible for the salvation of certain friends and relatives.

'I prayed for these people, but I also felt I should be on my toes to say something that would be effective for their salvation. That was a tremendous amount of pressure, and their salvation weighed heavy on me. It was a great burden,' Leanne explained.

'Gradually, I came to realise that everything I am and am not is my own choice. I also came to realise that these other adults have the same option of whether or not to be concerned over their salvation.' She concludes, 'I think I am a more effective witness now. Instead of praying and watching and waiting to have a specific conversation with someone, I am living my life in a day-to-day manner to show I appreciate the gift of life that God has blessed us with. Also, I have given up the responsibility of "converter" and am allowing room for the Holy Spirit to work.'

The Paradox of Running

When God spoke to Jonah, that scared prophet of doom went in the opposite direction. Instead of solving his problems, he actually made them worse. In *No More Mr Nice Guy* Stephen Brown describes this as a strange paradox. He points out that when you are afraid to make waves for Christ and you hide from a particular issue, your anxiety level actually rises. On the other hand, when you choose to stand, God stands with you.

> Whatever you have learned or received or heard from me, or seen in me – put it into practice. And the God of peace will be with you. (Phil. 4:9)

> Have I not commanded you? Be strong and courageous. Do not be terrified; do not be discouraged, for the LORD your God will be with you wherever you go. (Josh. 1:9)

At a conference for women's ministries one speaker, Luci Swindoll, talked about taking risks for Christ. She said, 'Become intentionally involved with people. Say yes when you are asked to do something. It will keep you young. If you hang up, they hang up. Then they will back off, and you will back off.

'When you take a risk, you don't have to look any farther than right in front of you,' she advised. 'If you look too far down the road you will get scared. Just keep your eye on the immediate. Our work is before us. We must determine how we respond.'

15

Witnessing Examples from Analysers

Analysers, like the other three personalities we have looked at, have their own set of excuses, fears and hangups about witnessing. Insecurity is a big issue for analysers. As they strive for perfection in every aspect of life, they tend to believe Satan's favourite lie that you can't witness until you can pass for the angel Gabriel's twin! Instead of falling prey to this line, analysers must dig deep to uncover God's special gifts, both spiritual and physical.

What Gifts Are You Hiding?

When our son turned eleven, we held a sleepover party for seven of his friends. Since that age group easily flops back and forth between being little boys one minute and teenagers the next, our big issue was whether to play party games. Jason finally decided it would be 'cool' to play a few during the calm minutes before the pizza was ready. The next problem was to dream up those 'cool' games.

Our analyser friend Dave was on hand to help supervise the chaotic evening. He suggested each boy should stand up individually to plead for his life, giving us all the reasons he should be allowed to live. The boys were to pretend we were their parents and then tell us all of their good points. Even for eleven-year-old boys, this was a soul-searching challenge not easily tackled!

What reasons would you give your parents? your spouse? your heavenly Father? Are you slumping down in a back pew to hide from the tasks God is calling you to tackle? Poinsettia plants may flower back to vibrant red in a dark cupboard, but spiritual gifts that lead to spiritual fruits are more likely to wither away when kept under cover.

Take a few minutes and write down a dozen personal gifts you have that can be used in God's service. While you are searching your heart, keep in mind Paul's advice: 'In everything give thanks' (1 Thess. 5:18 NKJV). Stick the list on the wardrobe door in your bedroom or on the bathroom mirror. Let the list serve as a quiet reminder that you do have what it takes to answer God's call.

Fighting Fear of Failure

With the analyser's inborn penchant for perfection, fear of failure in witnessing is just one more fear to overcome. Analyser Christians would benefit from sticking up on their refrigerator door some of the favourite sayings master sales-trainer Tom Hopkins uses to help salespeople overcome fear of failure. Try these, for example:

I never see failure as failure . . .

but as a learning experience.

but as the negative feedback to change course in my direction.

but as the opportunity to practise my techniques and perfect my performance.

Tom's Champion's Creed for all salespeople also touches a nerve for the analyser who hesitates to witness. It reads: 'I am not judged by the number of times I fail, but by the number of times I succeed. And the number of times I succeed is in direct proportion to the number of times I try, with the possibility that I may fail.'

Every word you utter is not going to send friends and family running down the aisle to kneel before the Lord. Jesus told us to expect rejection and persecution: 'Blessed are you when men hate you, when they exclude you and insult you and reject your name as evil, because of the Son of Man. Rejoice in that day and leap for joy, because great is your reward in heaven. For that is how their fathers treated the prophets' (Luke 6:22–23).

For the analyser to expect every word and every deed to have 100 per cent success is so unrealistic it is ridiculous. The issue is not that of being a 'witnessing failure' as much as of 'failing to witness'.

Getting a Good Start

Pastor John Maxwell said, 'All witnessing begins with character – with the decision to witness because it is the right thing to do. If we wait until we *feel* like it, we will never get started. All great soul winners begin with the character decision to make a commitment.' That's because once you *decide* to obey Christ's command to witness because it's the right thing to do, you won't allow a few mistakes to hold you back.

At a worship service another pastor used two stories to illustrate this fear of not being quite good enough for God. With children gathered on the steps at the front of the sanctuary, he compared our spiritual gifts to a box of crayons. When he was a child and received a new box of sixty-four Crayola crayons, he didn't want to use them because they would eventually get broken and messy. He asked the children to think about all the great pictures that would never be created if the box of crayons was never used. Whatever pictures came out of those crayons, he said, would be much better than the crayons themselves. Then he asked, 'Are there any gifts that you are afraid to use for God because you're afraid you'll use them all up or that they won't be good enough?' We might well consider our unused gifts as our personal box of crayons.

The pastor directed his second story to adults. 'A farmer found an eagle's egg and put it under a chicken. The eagle hatched and was treated like a baby chick. It grew up as a chicken, scratching in the ground for worms and using its wings to flutter only a few feet across the ground.

'One day the eagle looked up and saw a magnificent bird gently soaring across the sky. Awed by its strength and grace, he asked a chicken what type of bird it was. The chicken replied, "That is an eagle, the strongest bird there is. He belongs to the air, and we belong to the ground." So the eagle lived and died a chicken because he never stretched his wings to fly.' The pastor challenged his flock, 'Take a chance – look up – stretch your wings.'

Don't Wait Until You Have All the Answers

One of the most common excuses analysers give for not getting involved is that they are not quite ready. They don't have quite enough information. They haven't had quite enough time to process everything. They are not quite sure they have all their beliefs lined up in a neat little row. For some reason analysers think they must jump off the high diving-board before they even know how to dog-paddle.

Seth has had twelve years of church school and the religious education classes that included, but he is still insecure about participating in a family Bible study because he is afraid his more outspoken wife will outdo him. It is not that he doesn't know or couldn't find the answers to whatever questions come up. Typical of analysers, he is afraid of *not* knowing and then being embarrassed about looking stupid. (Remember that where a director wants to be in control, an entertainer wants to be liked and a peace-keeper wants to go with the flow, an analyser wants to be knowledgeable.)

Using the excuse that your faith is too new or too tender can grow into a terminal stall. You can procrastinate a long time unless you define 'too new' or 'too tender' in specific terms. Do you think you should be a Christian for a week, a month, a year, a decade or a lifetime before you begin witnessing? Do you need to have read the Bible cover to cover at least once? A dozen times? Do you need a year of perfect attendance at church? What specific changes would you like to see in your faith before you begin to witness? You must define what is holding you back, and then take specific steps to reach that ideal you define, so you can get on with Jesus's commandment.

Whatever you do, don't wait until you are your image of 'perfect Christian'. Bruce Larson writes in *Living Beyond Our Fears*, 'If you wait to act until you have all you need to assure success, you've probably missed the magic moment.' When you get started doing *anything*, you can expect to do some learning along the way. It doesn't matter if you are planting a flower garden, raising a family, transferring to a new department at work, sharing your faith or learning to ski. It takes time to learn a new skill.

When Jason was four we put him on his first pair of skis.

It was a bitterly cold day just after a January thaw. The alternate melting and freezing had caused the mountain to become just like an ice-skating rink turned at a forty-five-degree angle. Four-year-old Jason didn't care that it was treacherous skiing weather. He was quite happy just standing on the skis, a few feet from the lodge, while his father gently pulled him across the frozen snow.

The next year he went down his first nursery slope, and the new few years he skied the intermediate terrain. As his competence caught up with the confidence that always seems to accompany youth, we let him loose to tackle the toughest trails of any mountain we skied. Now Jason takes on expert-only runs with names like Agony, Suicide Alley and White Heat, where, as one intermediate-level skier friend quipped, 'a priest is at the top giving the last rites'.

Jason worked through the progressive levels – practising, taking spills, mastering techniques, building confidence along the way – and only that allows him to take on the tough stuff and enjoy it.

God doesn't expect you to go out and teach a course on salvation to theology students. Look for the nursery slopes first. Don't wait until you can ski down the steepest trail, or you will never get started. If you sit and wait until you've learned the answers, life, as well as countless opportunities to serve God, will pass you by.

Curt, the customer-service specialist, says the best way to get involved in witnessing is *to get involved*. He was attending church only two or three times a year when his pastor asked him to teach the Sunday-school class for twelve to thirteen year olds. Curt says, 'I am always asking God to push me, to use me as a tool. I agreed to teach the class because, if a pastor finds a reason to seek me out and ask me, I thought it must have been God's will.

'The really funny thing is, I *needed* to teach year eight that year. I never paid attention in Sunday school. I was just like every one of the kids in my class when I was their age, even worse. The clever part is that the theme for the year was "According to God's Plan". What we were studying every Sunday morning strengthened my faith. It also opened my eyes, in many cases for the first time, to the miracles of faith presented in the Bible.'

Curt says now he looks for ways to 'wash feet' the way Christ would do in a minute for anyone he would meet. He says, 'It might be as simple as opening the door for someone or picking up litter, or it might be washing up at Christmas at a church serving meals for the homeless. I am looking for opportunities to serve others on a day-to-day basis without the others knowing what I'm doing or without making a big fuss about it.'

Putting It into Words

Charles Jones, author and businessman, has made it a point to share his faith with his professional peers. He suggests using a simple conversion conversation that states the Bible is true, Jesus is humanity's Saviour and God loves sinners. Jones will often simply say, 'If the Bible is wrong and you are right, a Christian has nothing to lose. But if the Bible is right and you are wrong, you have everything to lose. The Protestant, Jew and Catholic disagree on a lot of things, but they all agree on this: the Bible is the Word of God.' St Augustine puts it this way: 'If you believe what you like in the gospel and reject what you don't like, it is not the gospel you believe, but yourself.'

Terry, a university student, talks about his tentative beginnings in witnessing. 'Whenever there was a sermon on witnessing, it would make me feel like I hadn't been doing my share because I was not actively witnessing. Guilt was dumped on the congregation to share with everyone and anyone you came into contact with. Some people may be comfortable with that, but I think it scares most people off. Inside they are saying, "Oh no. Here comes John the Christian Converter." I know people who are like that. They are good Christians, and they mean well, but I just can't do that myself.'

To this analyser, the biggest turn-off is direct quoting. 'I used to think ten particular verses were very important and very critical. I was nervous that I would forget one. I was probably more worried about getting the information out than how it was being received.

'I think all those verses are good, but I also think they are scary. We need to point out God's love and talk about him on a more personal level. When you quote, it distances you from your listeners. I think you should leave quoting to academic papers complete with footnotes. When you are talking to someone, they want to talk to you and not to someone who is dead. They want to know *your* opinion.'

Lois explains that that opinion needs to be a *tempered* opinion. 'I have had to stop and weed out the bad things that I do that are not a good witness, particularly my tendency to be too critical. Through the years I have had to learn that I cannot push my opinion on others. I have finally realised that many of the times I have been critical have concerned situations I really had no firsthand experience with.' Lois says that now she doesn't share her opinion until she has had the chance to get a feeling for the people and the situation.

Lois takes her faith to the office, where she has helped many young people make purchases they would otherwise have to do without. 'I trust them and allow them to buy a sewing machine from me on easy terms,' she explains. 'I don't use a written contract or go through a finance company that would charge interest. It is strictly a verbal agreement, and I offer low payments that they can easily meet.

'This is a tangible, Christian-based concept. In some cases I offer this to people who have had a rough life. I haven't known them, but I trust them and encourage them. This seems to make a big difference in their lives.' Lois adds, 'More and more I also notice that I am bringing a very optimistic attitude to work. I was gone for a few weeks recently, and people said they missed my cheerfulness.'

Responding to a Crisis

The old adage 'Actions speak louder than words' is never more apparent than during the aftermath of a crisis. A car with four teenagers made a right-hand turn into the school car park and crashed head-on into a pickup truck. The driver survived, but two of her sixteen-year-old friends were killed. The small town was shattered by the tragic accident.

Many grief-stricken teenagers were drawn to seek comfort from one of the older students, a young man I had long admired for his strong faith in Christ. I asked him to talk about how his faith helped him meet the needs of these youngsters.

'I knew the girls who died were Christians, and that gave me strength,' he explained. 'The other kids felt comfortable coming to me because I wasn't an emotional basket case. Also, I didn't give them a load of pat answers like "Everything will be all right – they are in heaven now." The kids were sad. They didn't want their friends to be gone. I had to meet them on that level.'

He said the response from the parents of the deceased teenagers also became a profound witness. 'One father became so obsessed with the loss of his daughter that he hated the driver who had "killed" his daughter but had survived herself. Everyone avoided this man because he was so filled with hate. But the other parents were Christians. They phoned the driver right away and acted almost as a voice for their daughter. They told the girl they loved her and that they were praying for her. They told the grieving teenagers that they were Christians, that their daughter was too, and that they knew she had gone on to a better place. They didn't give it as a pat answer. They said they didn't want her there now, but that they knew she was happy.'

Just Be Yourself

Tom, an executive with a multi-national food company, talks about how he shares his faith. 'I used to be afraid to witness because I didn't want to embarrass myself or offend the other person because they didn't have the same beliefs or the same relationship with Christ. I felt it was similar to how each person has his or her own hair or clothing style. If you go and push your views on that person, you can so easily offend them. Now I've learned to witness by just talking about Christ from my perspective and from my experience.

'Everything has been a nudge. I didn't put on a robe and go and stand in the biggest square in the city and preach! The best way to start is to build up your own relationship with God,' advises Tom. 'Build your security in God. When you go to church, any church, look at it as a way of refuelling.

'You don't have to be eloquent to be a witness. You just have to have the Spirit of God in your heart. You simply have to share from your heart, and to stand up and be like Jeremiah. God will do the rest.'

Tom says that when he shares his faith with colleagues, he likens it to running. 'It's easy to compare my faith to running, because I like to run. When I'm talking to someone who can also relate to running, I tell him how I trained for the marathon. I'd knock off twenty or so miles at a time during December and January when it was bitterly cold. I hated it, but I knew the finish – the marathon itself – would be worth it. I explain that I feel that way about Christ. It may not be easy, but the finish – knocking at the gate and having Christ open it – will be worth it.'

Personality Witnessing Workshop

1. Write your personal testimony, in letter form, to an old friend.
2. List your ten best personality strengths.
3. List your ten worst tendencies.
4. Write a paragraph about how you see the Holy Spirit bridging the gap between your two lists.
5. List the people and events who have influenced your walk with Christ.
6. Using the examples from your own life as a guide, explain how you can witness for Christ.

16

So What Are You Waiting For?

One of the biggest problems with witnessing is getting, keeping and maintaining enthusiasm. Have you ever noticed how the longer you are involved in something, the more your enthusiasm starts to wane?

When I was seven I joined the local Brownie pack. I wore a sweet little brown dress with a brown bobble hat and brown knee-high socks. We met in the basement of the school one afternoon a week, and I tucked a coin in my shoe to pay the subs. My mother was a Brown Owl, and my older sister was also a member. I never stopped to think whether being a Brownie was the cool thing to do. Everyone I knew was in the pack, the meetings were fun, and I was happy.

A few years later, towards the end of my junior-school years, I rushed home from school to change into my Guide uniform. After all, I wouldn't dream of wearing it to school! By my mid-teens, a few short years later, the scene had changed considerably. The meetings were held one evening a week at a house one street from mine, the Ranger uniforms were ugly, and none of my close friends had stuck with Guiding because it just wasn't the thing to do. It was so uncool to be a Ranger that you didn't dare tell even your closest friends!

With an ounce more of self-confidence and an ounce less of peer pressure, I might have screwed up the courage to tell my friends that I hung on because the summer activities were fantastic. At one camp in a rural setting I went on cross-country bicycling trips, took canoe trips down the river, waded in the stream, hiked, went swimming and did all the other things that go with spending summers with a crowd of girls your age when out of earshot from your parents!

Fortunately, nothing in the Guide handbooks required members to tell their friends about Guiding. I could easily deflect any stray questions about the time I spent at weekly meetings during the school year. I just focused on the summer fun ahead and generally kept quiet about the organisation I had belonged to for ten years.

Being a Christian does not exempt one from this tendency to drop out. Think about it. When you first accepted Christ as your Lord and Saviour, you probably couldn't wait to tell the world. Then that world began cooling your passion with cold comments like 'Thanks, but no thanks.' After a while our automatic response is to leave witnessing to the professionals or to other church workers.

Christianity doesn't afford us the choice of whether to witness. Our handbook expressly says we must do so. You cannot be a secret disciple. 'If you confess [to others] with your mouth, "Jesus is Lord," and believe in your heart that God raised him from the dead, you will be saved. For it is with your heart that you believe and are justified, and it is with your mouth that you confess and are saved' (Rom. 10:9–10).

Jesus told the disciples they would be responsible for spreading the good news. In Matthew 10:27 Jesus said, 'What I tell you in the dark, speak in the daylight; what is whispered in your ear, proclaim from the roofs.' After Jesus had risen, he clarified this command. 'Go into all the world and preach the good news to all creation. Whoever believes and is baptised will be saved, but whoever does not believe will be condemned' (Mark 16:15–16).

The message is clear; we cannot be indifferent to the salvation of others.

A German pastor and victim of a Nazi concentration camp created a sort of parable revealing how indifference is a disease that creeps up slowly. When the Germans first came for the communists, he didn't speak up because he wasn't a communist. He didn't speak up when they came for the Jews because he wasn't a Jew. When they came for the trade unionists and then the Catholics and then the Protestants, he didn't say anything because he wasn't part of those groups either. When the Germans finally came for him, no one was left to object (from *Illustrations for Biblical Preaching*, p. 203).

We may choose to keep silent because we're not a church member or because the time isn't right or because we don't feel knowledgeable enough, but we may as well be telling God we are too busy to be bothered. Dante once said, 'The hottest places in hell are reserved for those who remain neutral in a time of great moral crisis.'

Analyser Curt says, 'We need to find the point between being too aggressive and too passive. Our number one consideration should be whether the idea or action is right or wrong. Full stop. If you believe something is morally wrong, you have an obligation to try to change it.' He adds, 'It is only when we Christians choose the hard road, which means throwing up our arms and saying, "I know this is right, and I am willing to do something about it," that we can begin to impact the world with God's love.

'The majority must stand up and make their feelings known. Right now, the majority are keeping quiet and the minority are the ruling voice.' Curt concludes, 'I finally decided to witness and to speak out because the realisation came to me, "If not me, who? If not now, when?" The buck must stop somewhere, and I realised it must stop here. With me. I decided I had to give witnessing a try.'

Personality Variety

We were never meant to take our one special ability and march into the world on our own. All the gifts and all the personality blends are interrelated and complementary. A diverse group of Christians joining together for one common goal is a strong witness in itself. One lone Christian working solo in a remote part of the world could easily be discounted as an isolated example. When the world sees how Christ has transformed the lives of whole groups of people, our witness has much more impact. Likewise, when one of us shirks and does not exercise his or her gifts, we present an improper and weak view of the reality of Jesus Christ.

> Just as there are many parts to our bodies, so it is with Christ's body. We are all parts of it, and it takes every one of us to make it complete, for we each have different work to do. So we belong to each other, and each needs all the others.
>
> God has given each of us the ability to do certain things well. So if God has given you the ability to prophesy, then prophesy whenever you can – as often as your faith is strong enough to receive a message from God. If your gift is that of serving others, serve them well. If you are a teacher, do a good job of teaching. If you are a preacher,

> see to it that your sermons are strong and helpful. If God has given you money, be generous in helping others with it. If God has given you administrative ability and put you in charge of the work of others, take the responsibility seriously. Those who offer comfort to the sorrowing should do so with Christian cheer. (Rom. 12:4–8 LB).

The beauty of all this variety is that we each have the freedom to be ourselves. God is calling us simply to be who we are. Nothing more. Nothing less. Just like the people who shared their stories with you here, you will know when you have finally allowed yourself to use your true gifts for Christ's ministry because when sharing your faith you will have the maximum amount of pleasure with a minimum of forced effort.

'Whatever your hand finds to do, do it with all your might' (Ecclesiastes 9:10). Thomas Edison once said, 'If we did half the things we were capable of doing, we would literally astonish ourselves.' With God directing our lives we are capable of even more. So stop the excuses and look for opportunities to talk about your relationship with Christ. And remember – tell it in a way that suits who you are. You'll astonish yourself!

Take Action

1. Write down the kind of witnessing you *don't* want to do.
2. Write down the type of service you *don't* feel comfortable doing.
3. Write down the kind of witnessing you know you *could* learn to do.
4. Write down the types of service you *could* learn to do and *could* enjoy doing.

5. Make the conscious decision to witness because it is the right thing to do and the only response to Jesus's command: 'Go and make disciples of all nations, baptising them in the name of the Father and of the Son and of the Holy Spirit' (Matt. 28:19).

Bibliography and Suggested Reading

Biblical Biographies

Deen, Edith, *All the Women in the Bible* (San Francisco: Harper & Row, 1983).

Mead, Frank S., *Who's Who in the Bible* (New York: Harper & Row, 1934).

Christian Apologetics

Friedman, Richard Elliott, *Who Wrote the Bible?* (New York: Harper & Row, 1987).

McDowell, Josh, *Evidence That Demands a Verdict*, Vol. 1 (San Bernardino, Calif.: Here's Life, 1991).

McDowell, Josh, and Stewart, Don, *Answers to Tough Questions Skeptics Ask About the Christian Faith* (San Bernardino, Calif.: Here's Life, 1980).

McDowell, Josh, and Wilson, Bill, *He Walked Among Us* (San Bernardino, Calif.: Here's Life, 1993).

Thomas, W. H. Griffith, *How We Got Our Bible* (Dallas: Dallas Seminary Press, 1984).

Faith Building

Augustine, *Confessions* (Westwood, N.J.: Barbour, 1984).

Chambers, Oswald, *My Utmost for His Highest* (New York: Dodd, Mead, 1979).

Frankl, Viktor, *Man's Search for Meaning* (New York: Pocket Books, 1946).

Kennedy, D. James, *Why I Believe* (Waco, Tex.: Word, 1980).

Lewis, C. S., *The Case for Christianity* (New York: Macmillan, 1943).

Lewis, C. S., *The Grand Miracle* (New York: Ballantine Books, 1970).

Little, Paul, *Know Why You Believe* (Downers Grove, Ill.: InterVarsity Press, 1988).

Richards, R. Scott, *Myths the World Taught Me* (Nashville: Thomas Nelson, 1991).

Ziglar, Zig, *Confessions of a Happy Christian* (New York: Bantam, 1978).

Personality Styles

Cathcart, Jim, *Relationship Selling* (New York: Putnam, 1990).

Kroeger, Otto, *Type Talk at Work: How the Sixteen Personality Types Determine Your Success on the Job* (New York: Delacorte, 1993).

LaHaye, Tim, *Spirit-Controlled Temperament* (Wheaton, Ill.: Tyndale House, 1992).

Littauer, Florence, *Dare to Dream* (Waco, Tex.: Word, 1991).

Littauer, Florence, *Personality Plus* (Grand Rapids, Mich.: Baker Book House, 1992).

Oswald, Roy M., and Kroeger, Otto, *Personality Type and Religious Leadership* (Washington, D.C.: Alban Institute, 1988).

Witnessing

The Book. Special edition of *The Living Bible* (Wheaton, Ill.: Tyndale House, 1971).

Bright, Bill, *Witnessing Without Fear* (San Bernardino, Calif.: Here's Life, 1987).

Brown, Stephen, *If God Is in Charge* (Nashville: Thomas Nelson, 1983).

Brown, Stephen, *No More Mr Nice Guy* (Nashville: Thomas Nelson, 1986).

Little, Paul, *How to Give Away Your Faith* (Downers Grove, Ill.: InterVarsity Press, 1988).

Petersen, Jim, *Living Proof: Sharing the Gospel Naturally* (Colorado Springs, Colo.: NavPress, 1989).